reviewing
leadership

Engaging Culture

WILLIAM A. DYRNESS
AND ROBERT K. JOHNSTON,
SERIES EDITORS

The Engaging Culture series is designed
to help Christians respond with theological discernment to our contemporary culture. Each volume explores
particular cultural expressions, seeking
to discover God's presence in the world
and to involve readers in sympathetic
dialogue and active discipleship. These
books encourage neither an uninformed
rejection nor an uncritical embrace of
culture, but active engagement informed
by theological reflection.

reviewing
leadership

a christian evaluation of current approaches

robert banks
and bernice m. ledbetter

foreword by max de pree

Baker Academic
a division of Baker Publishing Group
Grand Rapids, Michigan

© 2004 by Robert Banks and Bernice M. Ledbetter

Published by Baker Academic
a division of Baker Publishing Group
P.O. Box 6287, Grand Rapids, MI 49516-6287
www.bakeracademic.com

Printed in the United States of America

Library of Congress Cataloging-in-Publication Data
Banks, Robert J.
    Reviewing leadership : a Christian evaluation of current approaches / Robert Banks and Bernice M. Ledbetter.
        p.   cm.
    Includes bibliographical references and index.
    ISBN 10: 0-8010-2690-3 (pbk.)
    ISBN 978-0-8010-2690-4 (pbk.)
    1. Leadership—Religious aspects—Christianity. I. Ledbetter, Bernice M. II. Title.
BV4597.53.L43B36 2004
253—dc22   2003025534

To
our friend and mentor, Max De Pree,
who taught us a great deal about leadership
through his writings, example, and influence

contents

foreword

I don't read many books on leadership, but the practice of good and ethical leadership is something I have thought a lot about. During my years at Herman Miller, Inc., especially as CEO, I tried to integrate my work and my faith—that's always been important to me and still is.

This book surveys the evolution of understanding about leadership and asks important questions about faith and leading that are necessary to consider if leadership is to have a future. I have come to believe that asking the right questions may be more important than getting to the answer. Questions help us bring to the surface what is most important, and this book does just that.

Reviewing Leadership helps us gain an understanding of the influences on leadership, things such as culture, timing, events in one's personal history, and one's faith. Leadership is a complex enterprise, and we do well to pay attention to influencing factors.

Peter Drucker once said that leadership and faith share a common core. They are both acts of intention, and this leads to integrity. Integrity in leadership is at an all-time low, and people need a reason to trust in leadership once again. Leadership is barren and hollow when it does not have integrity at its core. The examples of faithful leaders offered in *Reviewing Leadership* give us good reason to hope that the core of leadership remains intact for those leaders who fight the good fight of faith and remain strong.

The authors of this book are right to discuss the spiritual importance of leadership, which cannot be overstated. Leadership has always had a spiritual dimension, and now is the time to underscore the importance of this vital leadership component. Good, effective, moral leaders have a compass, something that guides them from the inside out, and faith is a good candidate for providing a clear set of moral principles to guide one's leading and following. The authors touch on the vital importance of the character of a leader by discussing the ripple effect of leadership on people, projects, and processes in organizations. In fact, the character of a leader may be one of the most important factors in determining the success of an organization because it really does spread throughout an entire organization, helping it to be beautifully whole or sadly fractured and broken.

Reviewing Leadership is a book about leading from one's spiritual center, which is the right thing to do and is not as easy as it sounds. It is really a journey of discovery about oneself and God and how one intends to lead based on who one intends to be.

The authors, whom I consider my friends, have offered some ways to think about this challenge that I encourage you to consider.

Max De Pree

preface

There are many books on leadership, and their number grows every year. This is as true within Christian circles as within the wider public arena. While most of these books discuss the nature, forms, and styles of leadership, they pay little attention to the popularity of such discussions. It is simply assumed that the interest in leadership is the result of its importance rather than particular cultural factors. Little attention is also given to a theological evaluation of current views on leadership, including those focusing on servant leadership, and of the adequacy of Christian treatments of the subject.

Although including a study of leadership in a series of books on contemporary cultural issues initially looks strange, the topic of leadership has achieved such cultural prominence today that a volume devoted to it has a place alongside other books in this series. Like them, the book is also different from many others in how intentionally and substantially it develops a theological rather than a purely practical or even biblical assessment of the current literature. It does this from a biblical base and with the conviction that what is best theologically ultimately leads to what is best practically. As the old but little appreciated adage goes, There is nothing more hands-on than a good theory.

This study of leadership has a particular shape. It is a summary of academic approaches and concrete experiences. It is a fruit of biblical investigation and reflection on our own experiences. It is an exercise in cultural analysis and theological exploration. It is derived from current writings on leadership and personal observations of exemplary role models. It has its basis in common sense and familiar proverbs and our exposure to film and poetry. Behind this diverse range of influences lie the convictions that, however normative biblical revelation may be, truth comes from God in a variety of ways and that all truth is God's truth.

These convictions have also shaped the form of the book. Though the book reviews recent writings on the subject, it also considers some historical figures and movements to give a sense of balance and perspective. Though most of the book has the character of analysis and argument, it also includes a number of anecdotes and illustrations from the workplace. These seek to give a more tangible and concrete shape to the ideas and principles. Though the book suggests guidelines and recommendations for action, it incorporates well-chosen personal stories and case studies from public life, for often these convey in more compelling form the heart and depth of what we are trying to say. In other words, we have sought to provide right-brain as well as left-brain elements in what we have written.

The opening chapter begins by asking about the wide and growing interest in leadership and whether there is anything distinctive about this. It attempts to provide a definition of leadership and seeks to distinguish it from management. As well as providing examples of what makes leadership problematic today, it lays out the key parameters for understanding leadership and highlights the importance of gender issues.

The second chapter offers a brief historical perspective on leadership, beginning with Paul's innovative understanding and practice. It then surveys historical models of leadership in the church, each containing a theological dimension, that may have application for today. The chapter also provides an overview of research on leadership throughout the last century and glances at the understanding contained in some popular writings.

The third chapter explores the rise of an implicit spiritual dimension in the literature on work in general and leadership in particular. After addressing explicit approaches to spirituality and leadership, it discusses specifically Christian approaches.

The fourth chapter begins by surveying a number of popular writings on leadership that include an overtly religious dimension. From this it moves on to discuss the strengths and weaknesses of a number of leading theological perspectives on leadership—revolving around Jesus, the Trinity, or biblical life stories—that form the basis for more systematic approaches.

The fifth chapter discusses translating ideas about leadership into practice. It examines the roles of imagination, emotion, and intelligence and then turns to three key aspects of character: faithfulness, integrity, and a servant-like attitude.

The last chapter considers some exemplary role models of Christian leadership. These include national leadership, leadership in a parachurch context, leadership in the city, leadership in the marketplace and the wider community, and leadership in a congregation. These case studies demonstrate the potential Christians have in various walks of life to articulate and embody a distinctive and integrated Christian approach. The book concludes with some reflections on how to nurture leadership of this kind for the future.

In writing this book, we want to acknowledge the opportunity given to us to exercise leadership in certain areas at Fuller Theological Seminary, especially our joint association in developing and codirecting the De Pree Leadership Center in Pasadena. We also want to acknowledge the experience and teaching opportunity we have had through the Macquarie Christian Studies Institute, Sydney, Australia, and the George L. Graziadio School of Business and Management at Pepperdine University, Malibu, California. For his generous provision of his course booklist, itself a work in progress, around which we built our own bibliography, we are especially grateful to our good friend Pat Lattore, who for more than a decade has taught courses in leadership to graduate theological students. We also want to acknowledge and express our appreciation to the series editors, Bill Dyrness and Robert Johnston of Fuller Seminary, as well as our acquisitions editor at Baker Book House, Robert N. Hosack. We are grateful for their understanding of our changing circumstances and for graciously granting us extra time to complete this manuscript.

the growing interest in leadership today

Definitions, Causes, and Issues

Talk about leadership abounds today. Voices on many sides deplore its absence or mediocrity, betrayal or corruption. The young are suspicious of it, the middle-aged tend to resent it, and the elderly long for it. Articles in newspapers and magazines, material in surveys and reports, and titles of popular and serious books highlight leadership as an important issue. A growing band of consultants offers advice on developing it, new centers focusing on various aspects of leadership continue to appear, and every year a regular round of seminars, workshops, and conferences features well-known experts in the field. It would seem, then, that leadership has become a leitmotiv of our culture, one of its pivotal concerns. The topic has become an integral part of intellectual and everyday discourse.

It would be easy to assume that this has always been the case. To one degree or another, every age has probably exhibited some interest in leaders. It had to, for sometimes it lived or died, or at other times was better or worse off, at the hands of such people. Even when people had little power over who led them—in the village, city, or country—it paid to know who was in charge and what they might do. But the current fascination with the subject goes far beyond this. It involves not just leaders as such but wider concerns about leadership itself. While this is not the first time reflection on the nature, scope, methods, styles, goals, and outcomes of leadership has arisen, there is arguably a broader and more systematic interest in the topic today than in any time past.

If this is the case, it prompts a series of questions. First, why is there, comparatively speaking, such a preoccupation with leadership today? When does a concern with leadership tend to surface, or is it a relatively constant affair? From whom does the main interest come—a particular group, class, or ethnicity—or is it widespread across the population? What personal, social, and cultural factors lie at its heart? Second, what key dimensions of leadership require attention today? What arenas of life—family, school, church, community, business, politics—are most in view when considering leadership, or does an interest in it appear across the board? How much is leadership an intriguing or a disturbing feature of social life? Does culture have the greater influence on the way leadership is understood and implemented, or do the views and methods of leadership have a greater influence on culture? This book, of course, is particularly concerned with whether Christians' core convictions shape their views and practices of leadership or whether these are more affected by wider cultural assumptions.

What Is Leadership?

AN ATTEMPT AT A DEFINITION

A common way of defining leadership begins with the person of the leader. This approach seeks to identify certain characteristics of personality (such as decisiveness or confidence) or style (such as collegial or confrontational) that leaders possess. This method, however, is too narrow and by no means always accurate. Leaders have many personality types and display a variety of stylistic approaches. It is in and through this array of forms that leadership expresses itself.

Another way of defining leadership is in terms of certain positions or status. Yet leadership is often exercised by people informally as well as formally, at various levels in an organization or group, and at times from the sidelines or in the background.

Another definition involves the influence leaders have on those around them. The difficulty here is the assumption that influencing others and acquiring followers depend primarily on leaders' personalities, gifts, or abilities. This is not always the case, for influence may spring from extraneous factors.

A final definition concerns the observable results leadership achieves. Leaders make decisions and get things done. Yet at the same time, though there is an inextricable link between leadership and results, some results are not immediate, and some leadership decisions are not supported or implemented.

In sum, then, leadership involves a person, group, or organization who shows the way in an area of life—whether in the short- or the long-term—and in doing so both influences and empowers enough people to bring about change in that area. Such leadership may be good or bad depending on the leader's style and the content of what the leader is advocating. From a Christian point of view, it is only when the direction and the method are in line with God's purposes, character, and ways of operating that godly leadership takes place.

LEADERSHIP AND MANAGEMENT

Leadership and management are two distinct yet related systems of action, and both are necessary for organizational well-being. They are similar in that each involves influence as a way to move ideas forward, and both involve working with people. Both are also concerned with end results. Yet the overriding functions of leadership and management are distinct. Management is about coping with complexity—it is responsive. Leadership is about coping with change—it too is responsive, but mostly it is proactive. More chaos demands more management, and more change always demands more leadership. In general, the purpose of management is to provide order and consistency to organizations, while the primary function of leadership is to produce change and movement. Management is about seeking order and stability, whereas leadership is about seeking adaptive and constructive change.[1]

Many organizations today are overmanaged and underled. But while improving their ability to lead, organizations should remember that strong leadership with weak management is no better and is sometimes actually worse. The real challenge is to combine strong leadership and strong management and to use each to balance the other.

As already mentioned, managers seek to bring order and consistency out of chaos and complexity. Managers manage complexity by planning and budgeting—setting targets or goals for the future. Such planning seeks to produce results that promote order in organizational structures and systems. By contrast, leaders deal with change, creating it, responding to it, or leading it. Leading organizational change begins with setting a direction and a strategy—developing a vision for the future along with strategies for accomplishing that vision.[2] Leaders set a direction by collecting information and data both within and outside the organization, looking for patterns, relationships, and links. Leaders watch the big picture and monitor factors such as market changes, key trends, competitors, and market share. Leaders watch internal indicators such as performance, the growth or decline of a product or service, and costs. Leaders also pay attention to organizational processes such as innovation and the morale of people in the organization. Managerial planning compliments the leadership role of strategic direction setting. Both work hand in hand to support the goals of the organization. Planning helps ground the direction setting in reality by asking, Can this plan be implemented? Is it

nd reasonable? Do we have the tools and the resources to turn this
  into a reality?

Managers achieve their goals by organizing and staffing. This includes various functions such as creating an organizational structure, staffing jobs with qualified individuals, and devising systems to monitor implementation. Management is concerned with creating human systems that can implement plans with precision and efficiency. Numerous decisions go into implementing any type of organizational system. These organizational decisions are not unlike architectural decisions. They are the blueprints of how work will transpire in an organization.

The counterpart leadership activity is aligning people. Leaders communicate the vision for an organization and the values that support the vision. They also translate the vision and the values into understandable and attainable acts and behaviors. They then help to create coalitions of people who can bring their passions into alignment in carrying out the vision. Aligning is more about communication and less about design. People should be able to infer an organization's core values without seeing them in print. These values define the organization and give it a soul. When outsiders can see the values of an organization in action, then that organization is aligned and powerfully positioned to excel.

Management ensures that a plan is accomplished by developing systems to control resources such as people, finances, and raw materials and through problem solving to deal with the unexpected. Managers are concerned with results and are charged with monitoring and measuring results by means of reports and other tools. Problem solving involves keeping plans on track, dealing with discrepancies, and redirecting resources. For leadership, achieving a vision requires motivating and inspiring people to stay on board and move together toward a common goal. To do this well, a leader must recognize basic human needs such as the need to make a meaningful contribution and to belong. Individuals in an organization bring with them their values and deeply held beliefs, their aspirations and desires to achieve. Leaders who can acknowledge and tap into these sources of creativity and passion will find the fuel needed to transform the idealism of their vision into a lived reality.

This last idea may be the point at which management and leadership diverge most dramatically. A leader's role in motivating and inspiring cannot be taken too lightly, for this is where follower and leader come together. Followers want their work to be motivating and their leaders to be inspiring. An effective leader operates at what James Clawson calls level three leadership, where the thoughts, beliefs, and feelings of followers are received and factored into the work an organization undertakes as its mission.[3] Level three leaders acknowledge and accept that people have passions and recognize the unlimited potential of the human enterprise when passion is brought to bear in an organization. So much of work is passion-free, void of real life-giving spirit. Tapping into the beliefs, thoughts, and feelings of followers invites the power of the human spirit into the workplace as a source of great energy and joy. If the human spirit was created to join with the Holy Spirit, it follows that when people can bring their full being into the workplace, there too is found the Holy Spirit.

It is easy for a discussion of the differences between management and leadership to become a delineation between good and better, with management being good and leadership being better. Both leadership and management are needed, however, for organizations and, most importantly, for the people in those organizations to do their work in effective, productive, and life-giving ways. Consider the following key roles of a manager and the tasks that fall under each role.

- A manager has an interpersonal role in which he or she sometimes acts as a figurehead and in this function may be seen as a leader. A manager's interpersonal role also carries with it the task of serving as a liaison among various groups within and even outside the organization.
- Because managers are involved in the flow of communication within an organization, a manager acts as a monitor, disseminator, and spokesperson of information. A manager constantly takes in new data, assimilates it, and then disseminates it through the appropriate channels. Good managers seek formal and informal ways to share information.
- The third key role a manager plays is the decisional role. A manager is at times an entrepreneur, at other times a disturbance handler, a resource allocator, and a negotiator. These functions all involve decision making.

These three managerial roles—interpersonal, informational, and decisional— and the functions that fall under these roles paint a picture of a complex, unboundaried, and demanding position. Henry Mintzberg, who developed these categories, reveals the immense challenge faced by managers to perform their jobs well. He writes, "The pressures of the job drive the manager to take on too much work, encourage interruption, respond quickly to every stimulus, seek the tangible and avoid the abstract, make decisions in small increments and do everything abruptly."[4] The role of manager involves many details and much responsibility and carries with it high expectations from those who depend on managers to perform their tasks well, on time, and with technical excellence.

It may be that leaders have more in common with artists, scientists, and other creative thinkers than do managers. Max De Pree states that leadership is like art. It is created and creative and at times improvisational, much like the music of a jazz band. Leaders begin with a design and then work with that design to change it while staying within certain boundaries of harmony, tone, tempo, and character. Leaders are like artists and other gifted people, which is why followers may feel they are sometimes impulsive and disorderly.[5] Abraham Zaleznik suggests that "leaders often experience their talent as restlessness, as a desire to upset other people's apple carts, an impelling need to 'do things better.' As a consequence, a leader may not create a stable working environment; rather she may create a chaotic workplace, with highly charged emotional peaks and valleys."[6]

Perhaps, then, leaders are the artists—designing, creating, and composing something new and original—while managers are the craft persons who work with the leaders' designs to add the finishing touches. They make the leaders' visions operational. Managers work with systems and people within an organization to create greater efficiency. They might be prone to say, "If it ain't broke, don't fix it." Leaders understand a different truth, "When it ain't broke may be the only time you can fix it," for leaders change the way people think about what is possible.

We should not overlook the fact, however, that despite their differences, managers and leaders are on a spectrum rather than on either side of a line. Most leadership positions require a degree of managerial ability, and some managerial positions contain possibilities for the exercise of leadership. Neither people nor jobs fall neatly into one category or the other.

Taking the Pulse of Interest in Leadership Today

Cultural analysts have occasionally examined the reasons behind the rise of a particular type of leadership. In the 1960s, for example, Theodor Adorno and others in the Frankfurt School of Social Research postulated that certain factors gave rise to "the authoritarian personality." This kind of person held positions of influence in the 1930s and 1940s during the rise of fascism and communism.[7] These researchers attempted to provide a theory that explained the influence of and the fascination with a certain form of leadership. Among writers on leadership and management, few have the breadth and the depth of cultural understanding to attempt such an analysis. Someone such as Peter Drucker, who brings into his work the European tradition and style of cultural reflection, has the capacity to do this and occasionally does so. Yet he is more concerned with the implications of broader social changes for the character of leadership than with why during some periods the topic of leadership is a central issue for a sizable portion of the population.

On the whole, there seems to be remarkably little reflection on the reasons underlying the current interest in leadership. There has been substantial investigation of the different attitudes toward leadership among the so-called builder (born before 1945), boomer (born between 1945 and 1960), and buster (born after 1960) generations. At most, such investigation reveals that a concern with leadership is more closely connected with the generation born in the third quarter of the twentieth century. Builders tend to take leadership for granted, whereas boomers tend to have serious doubts about it, though the latter's desire for better role models indicates a continuing latent interest. But the growing literature on generational attitudes rarely seeks to explain why there is a *preoccupation* with leadership. A spate of books has also examined what is wrong with the way leaders perform, but these tend to focus on the person of the leader. They do not look at the wider factors and pressures that might be involved and therefore do not raise questions about deeper cultural perceptions. Attempts have also been made across a range of occupations to discern changes that are—or should be—taking place in their typical styles of leadership. Such books have examined the world of politics, of business, of community organization, and of the church. Only rarely, however, do such attempts discuss why concern with these styles of leadership has become more prominent during the last couple of decades. At most, they suggest that the changes taking place in people's psyches and in social dynamics indicate the need to develop new paradigms and practices of leadership.

In what follows, we attempt to identify some of the key factors that could help explain the present interest in leadership. This is not offered as a definitive analysis or an exhaustive typology of the matter but as a general set of possibilities that might begin to explain this phenomenon.

People are usually concerned with leadership during times of crisis. Such was the case with Rudy Giuliani and his leadership in the aftermath of the attacks on the World Trade Center in New York City. Prior to the crisis, his image as a leader was declining as he awaited the completion of his term. On September 11, 2001, he soared politically, socially, and as a leader of the people, for the people, and by the people. His quick and decisive response to the terrorist attacks has been heralded as great, his public presence and communication "presidential." He will be remembered as the great leader of this moment in U.S. history.

In a time of war, there is likely to be strong interest in military leaders. In a time of widespread injustice, social and sometimes legal leaders capture people's attention. In a time of moral decay, people focus on ethical and even religious leaders. As the United States sought to find answers to the problem of evil manifested on September 11, Billy Graham reemerged as the representation of all that is good, moral, and Christian in a world bereft with grief and uncertainty. In a time of economic downturn, people look to business and commercial leaders. On the whole, people show less interest in leadership when things are going well. During such times, people may continue to show interest in heroes or celebrities, but they are rarely the ones to whom people look to get them out of a crisis.

An interest in leadership also tends to appear during periods of widespread uncertainty and rapid change. The local or international, social or economic, racial or cultural scene may be uncertain, causing people to feel anxious, unsettled, and insecure about the future. Or perhaps the pace of change is so fast or the changes so unpredictable that people feel things are out of control. Sometimes these concerns give rise to the desire for insightful and dependable leaders who can help people understand what is happening and how it affects them, as well as give them confidence in their present circumstances. At other times, the interest in leadership has more to do with the future than with the present. In such cases, talk turns to training leaders for the next generation.

A striking example of a group becoming concerned about leadership during a time of uncertainty took place in 1992 when Franco Bernabe was appointed CEO of Italy's large, energy-focused industrial group, ENI, and given the task of transforming the company. Bernabe reinvented ENI, formerly a government-owned company full of corruption, taking the company through a moral as well as a financial change. Bernabe envisioned a publicly held enterprise freed from unethical practices. Within thirty days of taking office, he issued the directive that everyone in the company would report directly to him. Next he called for the resignation of all top-level executives (many of whom had been indicted for unethical business practices). He sold off parts of the company that were no longer profitable and appointed those in lower management level positions with whom he had worked in the past to fill the executive openings. ENI was a company desperately in need of change and strong leadership. Bernabe filled the role and exceeded the expectations of his followers, seizing the moment of his appointment to take the company to a new level of moral and financial performance.[8]

Another factor that plays into a concern with leadership is the failure of particular leaders. This is especially the case when they are public figures of whom people have considerable expectations or on whose performance much depends. We live in a time when many leaders entrusted with important responsibilities in the public, social, and commercial sphere have committed sexual, moral, legal, or financial indiscretions. While, as in the case of President Clinton, their achievements may help them maintain a high public rating, their acts still contribute to greater cynicism about leaders and leadership in general. At such times, people analyze what is going wrong, make comparisons with other and better days, make recommendations about improving the situation, and call for better training of leaders. When a more endemic disillusion with leaders sets in, as among many young people today, there is the added problem of how to motivate them to take leaders seriously and to take on leadership roles themselves.

Jean Lipman-Blumen of Claremont Graduate University offers the following five reasons why we tolerate bad leaders. (1) It is too difficult and takes too much effort to unseat them. (2) We don't have enough support from others to challenge them, and we can't do this alone. (3) Overthrowing them is too risky. (4) More important issues and even crises need to be addressed. (5) They are not so bad after all, and at least we know what their faults are. Why is it that some leaders simply cannot lead well? They have an inability to assess themselves in realistic terms. The natural result of this inability is the attempt to overcompensate by creating perceived greatness through the exercise of power and greed. Further, leaders who believe they can lead "at a distance" too far away from the followers will eventually be brought down. These "distanced leaders" may try to create a false sense of harmony in exchange for the complex work of leadership, such as creating a vision and gaining a strong following to implement that vision. Over time such leaders become separated from the needs, wants, values, passions, and interests of their followers. At this point, followers abandon them. A "me first" agenda also lies at the root of the demise of leadership.[9]

Certain societies or groups in society appear to have a more ingrained interest in leadership. Such an interest may well have its roots in the historical situation and challenge out of which that society arose. This is arguably the case in America, whose citizens often find it difficult to understand that other societies do not accord leadership the same status. For example, in Australia, there is the long-standing and much discussed "tall poppy syndrome." Whenever anyone rises above the rest, particularly as a leader, people have a tendency to cut him or her down to size. It is often difficult to tell whether this springs from a sense of resentment or a desire for equality. Celebrities, at least in sports, and some homegrown entrepreneurs with a flair for philanthropy or self-demotion are partially excluded from this. This phenomenon also explains the Australian tendency, now diminishing, to favor the underdog over the anticipated winner. On the other hand, for all their overtly democratic rhetoric and character, Americans assume that no group or organization can exist without an appointed leader, who organizes and runs it, and that nothing can be achieved without a highly visible and structured leadership. This view causes a degree of on-going interest in leadership, whether or not a significant crisis or uncertainty is looming.

From time to time, certain groups in society whose ability to attain leadership in various fields is seriously restricted also begin to take a more pronounced interest in it. Throughout history, some social groups have been more disadvantaged than others. This is certainly the case with women and minority ethnic groups. During times of rising social expectations, a desire develops for a place in the sun and a stake in the positions of power that others have monopolized. As such groups begin to see the possibility of gaining more representation at the top, there is increasing discussion of the following issues: how to help this process escalate, what prevents it from taking place more quickly, and what differences in leadership goals and styles such people will or ought to bring. This development pushes the question of leadership into the foreground.

Another factor in some of the current fascination with leadership is the appearance of new types of leaders who have gained wide public acknowledgment or notoriety. These often fuel a new, or revive a declining, interest in the issue. In the last few decades, we have seen the rise of the titans of high finance, those who follow in the footsteps of the so-called captains of industry of the last century and the heads of corporations in the middle and latter part of this one. In the high-growth information technology area, we have seen the emergence of innovative younger leaders associated with Apple, Netscape, and Microsoft. Issues relating to rights—from civil to consumer to environmental—have produced a highly regarded, sometimes venerated, set of visionaries and strategists. In some areas, despite the continuing glass ceiling in many fields, women have risen to positions of preeminence, in doing so providing a new kind of role model for younger females in the workplace. The field of community organization has also given rise to new kinds of leaders who parallel celebrated religious figures who are involved in serving the poor and the disadvantaged. There has also been a series of impressive idealistic social and political figures, from Václav Havel to Nelson Mandela, who have found themselves in positions of unexpected power and have conducted themselves with considerable statesmanship and magnanimity.

Related to this phenomenon is the visibility and number of leadership institutes and centers, programs and courses, gurus and writings. While such entities exist in various places, nowhere do they do so on the same scale as in the United States. This is partly because of the greater preoccupation with leadership in this country, but other factors are also involved. For example, there has been an enormous increase in postgraduate programs in business and administration. There is also the continuing need of academics to colonize new fields of endeavor. Whatever the reasons, once leadership studies in universities and leadership programs through consultants and centers become entrenched in academia and the marketplace, discussion about leadership develops a momentum independent of other social and cultural factors. Indeed, it runs the danger of becoming a self-legitimating industry.

To conclude, when several of these factors come together at the same time in one person or group, they reinforce one another and carry the topic of leadership to new heights of public consciousness. This is what appears to be happening today.

Key Parameters for Understanding Leadership

A number of key parameters for understanding leadership—sometimes complementary and sometimes in fruitful tension—require attention. All too often, especially at the popular level, one or another aspect of a more complex parameter is singled out as if it comprises all that is important. This results in a narrow understanding of leadership. At other times, particular aspects of leadership are considered as if they were largely independent of one another. This underestimates the complexity that characterizes leadership. On occasion, discussions of leadership are too individualistic and do not give proper attention to significant relational, structural, or cultural components. This produces a one-dimensional portrait that is inadequate from both a descriptive and a prescriptive point of view.

First is the question of what words to use. What is primarily in mind here? Are we talking about leaders or leadership? A discussion of leaders keeps the focus on people, though doing so leaves some subsidiary questions up in the air. For example, are we talking about only the top person in an organizational setting, about the several people at the top, or about leaders in different parts of the organization, such as upper management, middle management, and lower management? A disadvantage of talking about leaders rather than leadership is that such a discussion may overlook organizations that are leaders and the influences they have on the people who lead them.

Using the term *leadership* enables us to look at the subject in a more systemic way, to investigate whether leading takes place through people who are not normally described as leaders. It also opens up the possibility of leaders emerging from a group, rather than being assigned the role of leader, as the members of the group grapple to make sense and meaning of their work.[10] A disadvantage of talking about leadership is that it may result in an abstract or theoretical discussion. While some writers suggest that we must choose between these two approaches, both terms have value and appropriateness. Indeed, both are needed to avoid their limitations.

There is also the question of the forms leadership takes. Often we discuss leadership only in terms of those who directly exercise it. But some people exercise leadership through others. The expression "the power behind the throne" conveys this state of affairs. At times this has been the only avenue open to disadvantaged people in society. Leadership is also sometimes viewed only in terms of those who hold formal positions within an organization. Formal—or positional—leadership revolves around the possession of title, recognition, or resources. Yet some people exercise leadership through the character and the competence they bring to a task and the recognition they acquire through the quality and effectiveness of what they do. According to Ronald Heifetz and others, informal leadership is the kind of leadership that works best in a network of organizations that is seeking to bring about change in a community.[11] This is because more formal kinds tend to be regarded by some organizations as attempts to arrogate a position or to control or manipulate a collegial enterprise. Grassroots leadership is effective in its ability to gain momentum and to effect change at various points simultaneously.

Both formal and informal types of leadership are necessary. Depending on the setting and the goal, one tends to have advantages over the other, though both are often needed to accomplish a particular task. In the climate of our times, a formal leader often needs the characteristics frequently associated with informal leadership to gain the recognition and collaboration of others. This is as true for pastoral ministry as for other professions.

In attempting to understand leadership, one must also address the nature of leadership. Is it a science or an art? For much of the last fifty years, many people assumed it was the former, and this is still the case in some circles today. From this point of view, leadership is essentially a matter of learning certain information, skills, and techniques. In recent years, others have challenged this assumption, arguing that leadership is more of an art form, like directing drama or playing music. There is truth in both positions. The second, however, requires more attention today because of the prevailing belief that a person becomes qualified for leadership through gaining certain formal qualifications, such as an MBA, or by going through certain training exercises designed to develop specific skills and abilities.

In response to this, we do well to see the act of leading as a process, as something that evolves and develops over time, rather than as an event fixed in time and space. This perspective allows us to evaluate leadership from a more open perspective, one that leaves room for creative expression and the ambiguity that naturally comes with unpredictability in the marketplace. At their best, leaders are able to combine the creative with the professional, the visionary with the logistical, the entrepreneurial with the managerial. At the very least, leaders surround themselves with and listen to people who complement their way of operating. In the end, we need to recognize that there is also an element of mystery to leadership. It refuses to open all its secrets to analysis, even of the most detailed and exacting kind. Genuine leaders expect and are at home with ambiguity, paradox, and even contradiction. They know that when these elements are not present, one can expect little flexibility, creativity, and innovation.

Understanding leadership also involves understanding the main types of leadership. Garry Wills identifies a number of types of leadership in his survey of significant public figures who arose at specific moments in history.[12] His list includes political or electoral leadership, military leadership, intellectual leadership, and socially transformative or what he calls radical leadership. Focusing on the church rather than public life, Bill Hybels lists ten manifestations of leadership. They include visionary, directional, strategic, managerial, motivational, pastoral, team-building, reforming, entrepreneurial, and networking leadership.[13] Such lists, which are by no means exhaustive, underline the fact that leadership is a highly complex and diverse phenomenon. They also show that "there is no one-size-fits-all approach to leadership. Leadership mantra #1: It all depends."[14] It is important to know, therefore, what kind of leadership is required in a particular setting at a particular time.

There is another dimension to understanding leadership. Too often people overlook the images embedded in their way of speaking about structures or rely too much on one or two dominant images. As Gareth Morgan suggests, organizations can be viewed as (1) machines or technical systems; (2) organisms within an environment; (3) brains or holographic systems, involving information processing and underlining the importance of their becoming learning organizations; (4) cultures, with their own ethos, stories, values, and symbols and containing subcultures of various kinds; (5) political systems, with a concern for governance, patterns of power, and capacity for conflict; and (6) interpersonal systems, whether healthy or dysfunctional, enabling or repressive, fearful or liberating. Only if the character of a particular organization is rightly understood can those in leadership develop the right kind of language and recommendations that will help the organization function effectively.[15]

The extent of leadership must also be examined. In the earliest decades of its analysis, leadership was often regarded as existing only at the top of an organization and, in a gradually diminishing way, at the head of the various levels of operation. More recent studies and experience suggest that it pervades organizations in a far broader way. It is, in fact, distributed throughout the workforce. Leadership takes place when someone shows how to excel at a specific task, questions an inefficient way of operating, gains the respect of others, cares for coworkers, makes a particular improvement, exhibits hospitality to marginal people or newcomers, or represents the best face of the organization to outsiders.

In the fall as geese head south for the winter, they always fly in a V formation. Studies of this pattern have shown that as each bird flaps its wings it creates an uplift for the bird next in line. By flying in this formation, the entire flock adds at least 70 percent to the distance an individual bird can fly. Whenever a bird drifts out of formation, it experiences the effect of trying to go it alone and promptly gets back in line. When the lead goose gets tired, it drops back in line, and another goose takes its place. In this way, each goose takes the lead at some point. Perhaps the activity of geese holds a lesson for leadership. While not all types of leadership or organizations can operate in this particular way, each person in a workplace is important and may have the potential to take the lead at a particular point.

One must also understand the levels and stages of leadership. With respect to the first, Elliott Jacques identifies a number of levels of authority, complexity, and skill. The number of levels present in an organization depends on its size and orientation. An organization typically involves the following: (1) Those whose work depends primarily on hands-on skill. Their goal is to do their work with quality and so give the lead to others. (2) Those who support and attend people at the first level as well as customers and clients. Their goal is service, which when maximized gives the lead to those around them. (3) Those involved in constructing, connecting, and fine-tuning systems. Their goal is to identify and implement the best practice in the organization. Those who help organizations attain this greatly enhance their capacity to achieve results. (4) Those, chiefly knowledge workers, who focus on inventing and modeling new futures. Their goal is to exhibit strategic capabilities that can show the way to others and the organization. (5) Those who overview organizational purpose within changing contexts. The subsequent redefining of mission can have wide repercussions for individual morale and organizational effectiveness. (6) Those who understand and interpret global contexts. They alert the strategic business units immediately below them to the wider business environment in which they work and must succeed. (7) Those who sustain long-term viability through high-level defining of values and molding of contexts. Such people provide the conditions that enable an organization to leave a legacy.[16] The key challenge for any organization—from a church to a corporation—is to know which levels are most relevant so that no pseudo-level is created or any important level overlooked. One of the dangers of understaffing, as well as the current fascination with downsizing, is that a key level is omitted with predictable results.

Overlapping with aspects of Jacques's typology but not identical to them is another typology that sets out the stages through which a person may pass during life with respect to leadership. For example, in young adulthood, people focus on serving an organization by performing their responsibilities as well as possible. In midlife, such people become more interested in making a real contribution through their work, and this sometimes requires courage as well as a spirit of service. In later life, these people begin to reflect on their legacy in the hope that their work will have a lasting impact on individuals or the organization. For this, genuine wisdom is critical. Leadership training needs to take account of these stages and develop specific learning opportunities and experiences for people entering or already operating at each level.

One also needs to understand the way different generations view and handle leadership today. Over the last decade, a number of qualitative and quantitative studies have explored attitudes to leadership among the so-called baby builders, baby boomers, and baby busters. Though it is unwise to generalize too much about the attitudes of people in these groups, certain differences do tend to appear. On the whole, baby builders have a more traditional approach to leadership. They are generally comfortable with a hierarchical or chain-of-command model, operating with clear lines of authority and delegation, and fairly fixed gender roles. For the baby builders, leadership dynamics are governed mainly by direction from above and obedience from below, sharing of knowledge operates primarily on a need-to-know basis, and promotion takes place chiefly up and through the system. This generation is still in power in many large institutions, though for some time it has been handing over the reins to the next generation.

For the most part, that next generation, the baby boomers, comes at leadership from a different angle. Instead of a hierarchical and chain-of-command model, they prefer one characterized by complementarity and circles of governance. While there is a clear place for leaders, and some positions are more central than others, their leadership style is more consultative and collegial. Teams, in which each member has a recognized contribution to make, play a greater role in getting things done. Embodying rather than simply giving direction, gaining others' buy-in rather than requiring obedience, a more open approach to sharing knowledge, and a flexible approach to promotion characterize this approach. It also tends to value a leader's personal awareness, relational skills, and ability to equip others more highly than the generation above it.

In the newer high-tech leisure and knowledge industries, the boomers have already begun to hand over the reins to the baby busters. What distinguishes this generation is a widely held aversion to leadership itself. They regard the more inclusive and user-friendly boomer model as too often rhetorical or promotional rather than genuine and therefore as superficial or manipulative rather than operational. They prefer a looser approach to leadership in which it rotates around a group rather than exists above it or even within it. Leadership takes the form of a network of groups with a significant degree of autonomy that operate in a more consensual way. Moving even further away from delegating and going beyond equipping, they talk of empowering all members of an organization to make a distinctive contribution to the degree that their gifts, wisdom, and imaginations enable them. When they do this, they exercise leadership, which is therefore a widespread rather than a limited resource.

Issues in Leadership

WOMEN AND LEADERSHIP

An important aspect of the growing interest in leadership today concerns women in leadership. In their book *Megatrends 2000,* John Naisbitt and Patricia Aburdene predicted that in the decade of the 1990s women would cease to be a minority in the marketplace. They said, "To be a leader in business today, it is no longer an advantage to have been socialized as a male. Although we do not fully realize it yet, men and women are on an equal playing field in corporate America."[17]

The role of women has indeed changed. Women have the freedom to choose a number of roles from stay-at-home mother to working woman with no children to any combination in between. But does a woman have equal status as a leader in the power structures of the workforce? It is well documented that the presence of women in leadership positions in the workforce increased and nearly tripled during the last three decades of the twentieth century.[18] At the same time, the number of women in top corporate leadership roles did not increase at the same rate. Only 1.1 percent of the top positions in the Fortune 1000 are occupied by women.[19] It seems that the perception of change is greater than the reality. Naisbitt and Aburdene forecast the ideal, but their prediction is not yet the reality.

Though a woman may feel called to express her gifts of leadership in the marketplace, she may also encounter resistance to do so. For women of faith, the issue of workplace equality also intersects with the question of vocational calling. The voices of women at the senior levels of leadership are still few, and it takes a great deal of courage and a clear sense of calling for women to make it to the table where key organizational decisions are made.

Deborah Swiss, an educationalist at Harvard University, suggests that "sometime in the last decade, the progress of women at work came to a quick halt, too many business leaders saying one thing but practicing another."[20] She surveyed 325 women representing a national cross section of professionals. Based on her survey results, Swiss identified the following facts about women at work:

- The salary gap mirrors the gender gap.
- Moving women into the managerial pipeline has done little to advance them into senior management/leadership positions.
- Gender, not talent, is often the deciding factor in who gains committee leadership or the golden client.
- Progressive policies on paper are meaningless in the absence of support from top management and line supervisors.
- An absence of objective performance standards against which everyone is judged perpetuates the double standard whereby women are held to a different standard than their male counterparts.
- For women, sexual harassment continues to be a silent partner in maintaining an unsupportive work environment.
- Gender bias, not parenting responsibilities, is the factor most likely to slow a woman's advancement.[21]

Swiss goes on to cite two important faulty theories as to why women are not advancing into the upper ranks of leadership: (1) The pipeline theory—allowing evolution to assume the burden of change, the notion that sheer numbers will make it impossible for gender to limit career potential—has minimal impact on the overall presence of women in leadership positions. The prevailing reality is that women need to work twice as hard and be twice as good just to stay even with men with the same credentials. (2) The work-family myth—that women will be able to advance professionally when organizations provide flexibility and services in support of mothering and other family responsibilities—also has minimal impact. Companies consistently ranked among the most "family friendly" have done little to shatter the glass ceiling.

On the topic of corporate culture and the way it can negatively affect women, Swiss notes that women who question the leadership style of command and control in favor of a more collaborative style can stifle their careers. Fortunately, many organizations are discovering the value of collaborative leadership, and this is gradually becoming the preferred style. For women in general, it tends to fit well; for the faith-based woman, leading from authentic collaboration has significant implications for creating organizational community.

When considering the need to position more women in positions of influence, we are talking about issues of diversity and change. In her book *Thinking in the Future Tense: Leadership Skills for a New Age*, Jennifer James states that diversity "is more than a policy. . . . It is our national identity and our unifying creed." We are "one nation of many cultures," and this is a "precursor of what lies ahead—one world of many cultures. . . . How well we accommodate diversity is indicative of how well we handle future change." Quoting essayist Asta Bowen, James suggests that within our country, "we are engaged in a pioneer effort to 'tune democracy to its finest tolerance,' and as leaders of faith, we are compelled to embrace and accept difference." More broadly, "we must make ourselves into global citizens, able to move easily among countries, currencies, languages, and customs."[22] Economic success in the twenty-first century will be highly dependent on our ability to come to terms with differences. She further calls for culture-free learning, that is, dispensing with the us-them mentality, as well as the need for individuals and organizations to develop "high diversity IQs."

By the year 2050, more than 60 percent of the U.S. workforce will be people of color, and more than 40 percent will be female. James points out the difficulty of being in a minority culture. At each new skill level, minorities find they must prove their competence. Yet when enough skills are demonstrated and are recognized, the majority begins to see the pragmatic value of diversity. The same is true for women. Regarding women in positions of power, James states that

> changing the work rules, changing the economic balance, and changing the division of labor changes everything at the deepest levels of society. The fear of these changes and the fear of women as equals seem to be worldwide, despite the success of Margaret Thatcher and Benazir Bhutto.[23]

Culture change goes deep into both individuals and organizations. To effect long-term meaningful change, "we have to rely on our own courage, [and] the best place to look for insight into managing diversity is inside yourself."[24] We could certainly add faith to the list. It takes courage, insight, and faith to embrace change and diversity. Women leaders of faith operate from a worldview of transformation. As God's intent is to bring about genuine change in the world through people of faith, it follows that the faith-driven woman leader will seek ways to transform systems so that diversity is recognized, honored, and celebrated. We might call this an aspect of the redemptive work of faith-based leadership.

CRITICAL TENSIONS

Faithful leadership in the marketplace begins with the question, Does faith make a difference in leadership? One way to answer this question is to see faith as the integrator of Christian values and business practices. Faith anchors leadership in deeply held beliefs about the world, people, and the purpose of work. In everyday practice, faith compels leaders to seek creative solutions to business challenges, solutions that are often not on the radar screen of business as usual.

Three of the key tensions leaders of faith regularly encounter are:

1. the tension between professional competence and being salt and light: seeking to be highly competent as a professional and knowing when it is appropriate to speak directly about one's faith in the secular marketplace
2. the tension between calling and trusting God: following the leading of God to serve as a leader and trusting God when situations do not seem to create the opportunity to follow one's calling
3. the tension between family and work: honoring multiple demands at home and pursuing integrity through and beyond the guilt many women feel at not doing enough for their significant others

As Laura Nash points out in *Believers in Business,* additional tensions leaders of faith encounter are between:

- pursuit of God and pursuit of power
- love and the competitive drive
- people's needs and profit obligations
- humility and the ego of success
- charity and wealth[25]

These polarities are the daily routine for leaders of faith, and faith is the glue that holds these polarities in tension. Accepting the journey of leading while living with these tensions is to understand what it means to be called, that is, finding a purpose of being in the world that is related to the purposes of God.[26] Faith and leadership meet where calling, values, and action come together. Does faith make a difference in leadership? The answer is clear: It must.

QUESTIONS OF POWER

Any discussion of leadership and faith must include the idea of power and how best to use power to move people, projects, and processes toward the accomplishment of goals. Janet Hagberg offers a well-integrated approach to the expression of power that works well for both women and men of faith. "Personal power is the extent to which one is able to link the outer capacity for action (external power) with the inner capacity for reflection (internal power)."[27] This idea brings together power and reflection so that a leader of faith can act thoughtfully, something that groups, teams, and organizations need.

Hagberg describes power as something that one grows into and that develops over time. Power tends to follow six distinct stages:

1. Powerlessness. At this stage, leaders can be described as secure and dependent, possibly trapped, helpless but not hopeless; fear holds them back from finding their true authentic power. At this stage, such people lead by force and inspire fear.
2. Power by association. This form of power comes about as leaders learn the ropes. There is some dependency on supervisors, and to grow, leaders must move out on their own, take risks, and develop competencies. Such leaders lead by seduction and inspire dependency.
3. Power by symbols. At this level, power is a controlling affair, and the people exercising it are often described as ambitious, competitive, charismatic, and egocentric. Not knowing they are stuck in this controlling stage of power holds them from going forward to the next stage. They lead by personal persuasion and inspire a winning attitude.
4. Power by reflection. Leaders at this stage use influence as a way to express their power. They are known for being strong, reflective, competent, and skilled at mentoring. They show good leadership by modeling integrity and inspiring hope.
5. Power by purpose. Leaders who express their power by purpose are known for their vision and can sometimes be called "the irregulars." This is because they are not ego oriented. They are quick to give away power and let others lead. They are self-accepting, calm, humble, confident of life's purpose, and spiritual. The hallmark of such leaders is empowerment, and this inspires love and service.
6. Power by gestalt. The final stage of power is expressed as wisdom. Leaders at this stage might be called the souls of the earth, for they are comfortable with paradox, unafraid of death, quiet in service, and ethical. In a sense, their power is almost invisible, and they seek to inspire inner peace in those around them.[28]

This model shows that the exercise of power moves from leader-focused power to other-focused influence. It allows leaders to see the promise of power when it is integrated with reflection in the service of others and not self. Leaders of faith can find in stages 4 through 6 the balance between the exercise of power and the personal integrity of faith.

Conclusion

Throughout any investigation of leadership, whether acknowledged or unacknowledged, is a central thread, the issue of values. The crisis that exists in leadership today is fundamentally a crisis of values. We cannot speak about leadership and ignore the values that are embedded in its very nature and expression. Leadership is not value-free, and to think so is to create a crisis in leadership. There is no neutral ground from which to examine leadership. The interactive nature of leadership inextricably touches people and their lives, thus calling leadership to a moral plane. "Leadership is a word that carries many hungers," remarked a Harvard Business School MBA student. Followers bring with them their wants, needs, aspirations, expectations, and hopes to the leader-follower relationship. Because of this, the word *leadership* and the act of leading carry with them the weight of responsibility that follower, leader, and organizational hungers will be addressed. The hunger inherent in leadership increases as change accelerates and the world becomes more global and less communal. Leaders must not only address these hungers and provide solutions but also seek to elevate the morality of leaders, followers, and organizations.

Within the issue of values, of course, lie core beliefs and worldviews, which ultimately drive attitudes, motivations, goals, and actions. It is at this point that a Christian perspective on life has its entry point and its relevance. A stark contrast can be drawn between God's and the world's view of leadership. Their relationship may be described as a tension between a purely business model of leadership and one based on biblical models and values. Or it may be expressed in terms of a control-based as opposed to a servant-oriented model of leadership.

Quite apart from the fact that the language of servant leadership had its origin in business circles—in the writings of Robert Greenleaf, who came from a Quaker background—this polarizing of positions suffers from other defects. In the first place, the church has been and still is riddled with leadership practices based on control, even in circles committed to leadership based on servanthood. Also, drawing too strong a contrast between Christian and worldly views overlooks the fact that God is active in the world through what has been called his general revelation and activity. Therefore, though the Bible is ultimately normative for and determinative of a Christian view of leadership, Christians should be open to any reflection of a genuine understanding of leadership that stems from other sources or traditions. What follows contains critiques of expressions of leadership in the church and even endorsements of leadership in the marketplace that contains echoes of a divine perspective.

biblical, historical, and contemporary perspectives on leadership

2

Although the first chapter touched on the modern study of leadership and some recent writings on leadership, before going on, we need to go back in time. This chapter identifies several of the main approaches to leadership practiced by Christians throughout the centuries. These approaches include those of the Benedictine, Lutheran, Presbyterian, Quaker, and Pentecostal traditions. Such approaches have their basis in an institutional setting—primarily the church or a religious order—that was influenced explicitly or implicitly by a particular set of theological convictions. While these traditions have often been examined for what they say about the nature and the pattern of ministry, such examinations have only rarely taken the broader issue of leadership into account.

To gain a more basic point of reference, however, it is important to go beyond these influential traditions and begin with the Bible, for the Bible provides the normative yardstick for investigating all major aspects of belief and life, including leadership. The focus here is on the New Testament. A later chapter considers an approach to some material in the Old Testament and draws additional conclusions from it.

A Biblical Benchmark: Paul on Leadership

Among the early Christians, Paul most clearly and fully articulates an understanding of leadership. Since he led a parachurch mission team and organization and set up local congregations in various cultural contexts, he also practiced leadership on a wide range of fronts. While Paul does not provide a systematic account of the nature and practice of leadership—indeed, he raises fundamental questions about its character and practice—he has much to contribute to a practical theological understanding. The following discussion considers how leaders functioned in the local churches, Paul's and his colleagues' roles in the churches, and Paul's role in the team that brought those churches into existence.[1]

LEADERSHIP IN THE LOCAL CHURCHES

For modern people, questions of governance are often of primary interest. Leadership is a central concern in any democratic and bureaucratic society. This is also the case in church life, which is more democratized and bureaucratic than in previous times. In social and religious arrangements, people prize order: It is not only a preoccupation but also a virtue, not only a means but also an end. As already noted, the issue of leadership influences attempts to understand chains of command and lines of authority. As a result, there is a danger of reading the priority we accord these matters into Paul's ideas about the church. He was certainly concerned about the church conducting itself in an orderly manner and about members being properly cared for and guided. But other than when a church's actions were inadequate, he says very little about such matters. For him, they appear to be secondary rather than primary issues.

The Language of Leadership

If we begin by looking simply at the basic words Paul uses in speaking about these issues, what strikes us first is the infrequency of terms related to those at the top, to formal power, and to organization. Of more than three dozen terms used of people in leadership positions in his day, the only high-ranking one Paul uses is in reference to Christ (Col. 1:18). Reference to order, or the need to be orderly, occurs infrequently in Paul's writings (1 Cor. 14:40; Col. 2:5), and only once is it clearly associated with the church, coming at the close of his instructions to the Corinthians about what should happen in their meetings (1 Cor. 14:13–40). Its opposite is *unruliness,* which is associated with disharmony (1 Cor. 14:33; cf. 2 Cor. 12:20). Paul never suggests that it is the role of one or a few people in the assembly to regulate its gatherings. This is everyone's responsibility as the people discern and share what the Spirit is saying (1 Cor. 12:7–11; 14:28, 30, 32). Organization stems from a highly participatory and charismatic process and is not determined in advance by a few. Likewise, the word *authority* rarely appears in Paul's writings. Only in two places does he use the word in regard to his own position—never in regard to those in leadership in local churches—and only then when his apostolic link with a church is being challenged (2 Cor. 10:8; 13:10). At Corinth, he certainly wishes to reestablish his unique relationship with the church as its founder (2 Corinthians 10–13), but he disassociates himself from the authoritarian way the "false apostles" conduct themselves. He does not seek to influence the members by improper means (2 Cor. 10:3), boast of his preeminence (2 Cor. 10:12–15), dazzle the church with rhetoric (2 Cor. 11:5–6), or manipulate and control his converts (2 Cor. 11:16–19; cf. 2 Cor. 1:24). His "authority" is exercised only for constructive purposes, and he prefers that the church take appropriate corrective action before he arrives so that he does not have to engage in it.

Basic Metaphors for Understanding Leadership

In talking about organization and authority, Paul draws on several metaphors to provide an overall frame of reference or paradigm for his view. Basic to this are metaphors and analogies drawn from family life. This is not surprising, for the language of family is the primary way of talking about the relationship between God and his people. Just as God is viewed as "Father" and believers as "children," so Paul describes himself as a "father" to his "offspring" in the faith (1 Cor. 4:14–15; 2 Cor. 12:14; 1 Thess. 2:11). This conveys an affectionate but responsible parental rather than patriarchal bond. Paul also speaks of himself as a "mother" who suffers labor pains (Gal. 4:19) and as a nurse who cares for her charges (1 Thess. 2:7; cf. 1 Cor. 3:2). This cluster of metaphors emphasizes both the affectionate relationship between Paul and his converts and his sense of responsibility for them. But it would be wrong to conclude that Paul encouraged a childlike dependency on him, for he treated believers as adult children and urged them to "grow up" in Christ and to become mature adults in the faith (e.g., 1 Cor. 14:20; Eph. 4:14). Other metaphors in Paul's writings, such as builder (1 Cor. 3:10–15) and farmer (1 Cor. 3:6–9), are drawn from the world of work and stress his fundamental role in starting and designing the Corinthian church. The metaphor of the body (1 Cor. 12:12–27; Eph. 4:1–16), especially the reference to the unifying and structuring role of the ligaments, reveals something about the central role of key people in the church whose primary responsibility is to help maintain unity and engender growth.

Participation in Leading the Gatherings

For Paul, what happens at church gatherings originates in the Spirit and flows through the entire membership for the benefit of all. Everyone is caught up in this divine operation (1 Cor. 12:7). The process itself is described through the use of action verbs that stress its dynamic character: Contributions to the meetings are "energized," "manifested," and "distributed" by the Spirit (1 Cor. 12:6–7, 11). Paul uses a variety of nouns to capture the diversity of what takes place. It is an exercise of "gifts," a variety of "services," different kinds of "working" (1 Cor. 12:4–6). The activities that result from these gifts highlight the diversity of the Spirit's working (Rom. 12:4–8; 1 Cor. 12:8–11; Eph. 4:11–13). Since, for Paul, everyone in the church is under an obligation to discern the validity of contributions to the meeting, this task is not in the hands of one person, a leadership team, or a worship committee, even if certain people play a more prominent role in shaping what takes place (1 Cor. 12:10; 14:30). While Paul provides some general guidelines for what should happen during a meeting (1 Cor. 13:1–3; 14:9–32; Eph. 4:12–15), if everyone respects these guidelines, there is no need for a planned order of service or for one person to lead it.

No Status Distinctions

Reference to certain people in the community playing a greater role than others leads to a consideration of key people within the churches. The language of priesthood appears only metaphorically in Paul's writings, never of a literal person or group, in regard to a wide range of devotional, compassionate, financial, and evangelistic activities (cf. Rom. 15:16, 27; 2 Cor. 9:12; Phil. 2:17, 25, 30). Paul's point is that the kinds of ceremonial activities God required of only some people in the Old Testament are now required of all Christians. This desacralizes and democratizes the role of those who have a significant part to play. The central corporate action in the churches was the Lord's Supper, which was held weekly and was a full, not a token, meal. Nowhere in Paul's letters, disputed or undisputed, is anyone identified as the official presider. This role probably fell to the host, in whose home the meal was held. If Paul's practice is at all typical, baptism also took place through other than leading figures in the movement (1 Cor. 1:14–17). As far as the usual terms for secular offices are concerned, only one of the more than thirty that existed in the first century appears in Paul's writings, but it is used exclusively of the governing role played by Christ in the church (Col. 1:18). Instead, the language of servanthood dominates. In the first century, however, this language did not necessarily conjure up ideas of lowly people undertaking inferior tasks. Servants of important social and political figures had considerable status and carried on high-level managerial and bureaucratic work. A servant's master determined that servant's status, and many servants had a higher social standing than free men or women who belonged to socially inferior families. In addition, because Christ is the Lord of Christians, their servant work has dignity and should be respected, and because he is the ultimate model of servanthood, he provides the profoundest example of how this should be undertaken.

Effective Functioning Rather Than Appointed Positions

On the whole, verbs rather than nouns are used more often in regard to those making a fundamental contribution to the church. What is crucial, therefore, are the functions people perform rather than the positions they occupy. For example, Paul refers to those who "work hard," "admonish," and "instruct" (Gal. 6:6; 1 Thess. 5:12) and to the way certain people proved themselves through conflict in the church (1 Cor. 11:19). When nouns are used, as of those who are "helpers" or "administrators" (1 Cor. 12:28), they tend to be used in regard to fairly ordinary rather than dramatic contributions. Apart from the pastoral letters (e.g., 1 Tim. 5:17), the term *elders,* referring to older, respected Christians who probably had a corporate responsibility for a cluster of churches in a city, does not occur in Paul's writings (but cf. Acts 14:23). The word *overseer* occurs just once and in the plural (Phil. 1:1), serving as a description rather than a title and as an ancillary to the "saints" in general. Ordination, as we know it, does not appear in the Pauline letters. The laying on of hands is mentioned, but this was used for such diverse procedures as giving the Spirit (Acts 8:17), healing from illness (Acts 9:17), and commissioning a person for itinerant service (Acts 13:2–3). While, according to Acts, Paul and Barnabas "appointed elders" in every church (Acts 14:23), this seems to have involved ratifying a community's choice, as was the case with the laying on of hands on the seven (Acts 6:3–6). When Paul identifies certain people in the church in Corinth as having a fundamental contribution to its life, he merely asks the congregation to "order themselves" under such people and instructs them to extend this attitude "to everyone who joins in the work, and labors at it" (1 Cor. 16:16). This suggests a nonformal, community recognition of a group, not an individual, that is based on the quality of the ministry people are already engaged in rather than on external qualifications.

Qualification of Family and Business Experience

As the pastoral letters indicate, people should be appointed overseers and helpers in the community only if they have first proven themselves in their households. But houses were workplaces as well as domestic spaces and involved the tasks of supervising slaves in addition to raising families. Proven experience and a good reputation in managing workers were therefore also qualifications for leadership in the church. It is not inappropriate to assume that this is the background for people singled out by Paul such as Titius Justus (Acts 18:7), Aquila and Priscilla (Rom. 16:3), Gaius (Rom. 16:23), Nympha (Col. 4:15), and Philemon and Apphia (Philem. 1–2). The social status of such people provided the basis for their having preeminence in the group, but only if, as Stephanas and his household did, they "devoted themselves to the service of the saints" (1 Cor. 16:15). This is not to say that in this case traditional authority replaced charismatic authority, for these people needed more than social status to qualify for this responsibility. What we find is an approach to authority that recognizes the charismatic gifts or social prominence of certain people but requires that other qualities such as commitment and servanthood also be present. Paul names women among this group, indicating that they often played a significant role in congregational life as well as among the itinerant group of apostles (Rom. 16:6–7) and prophets (1 Cor. 11:5). Women may also have operated as evangelists (Phil. 4:3), and among Paul's associates was a wife-and-husband team involved in at least occasional high-level instruction (Acts 18:26). Paul rises above the gender as well as the status distinctions of his time.

Motivating by Persuasion Rather Than by Command

Paul plays a visible role in the birth and ongoing life of the churches he founded. With other churches, he cannot and does not assume a preeminent position (cf. Rom. 1:11–13). Yet the day-to-day ordering and governing of affairs in the churches Paul founded lay in the hands of the congregations themselves. In churches in which things are going relatively well, such as the church at Philippi, Paul addresses problems without reminding believers of his foundational role in their lives or of his apostolic authority. In churches in which things are not going so well and his role is being challenged, such as the church at Corinth, Paul reminds his converts of his seminal role in the church's life (1 Cor. 4:15) and, from a distance at least, plays a more directive part in their affairs. But nowhere does he exhibit an authoritarian stance. He is more concerned that his converts "imitate" him rather than "obey" him (1 Cor. 11:1; Gal. 4:12; Phil. 3:17), and he instructs others by means of appeals (1 Cor. 4:16) based on love (Philem. 8–9) far more than by means of "commands" (cf. 1 Cor. 14:37). His few calls for obedience have to do with responding appropriately to his loving urgings (2 Cor. 2:9), remaining faithful to the gospel (Philem. 21; cf. Phil. 2:12), and yielding to the prompting of the Spirit (1 Thess. 4:8).

PAUL'S AND HIS COLLEAGUES' LEADERSHIP IN THE CHURCHES

Paul's Role in the Local Churches

The issues just discussed are in accord with certain characteristic features of Paul's method of operation. Since they have the gospel (1 Cor. 15:3), basic instruction (1 Thess. 4:1), Paul's own example (Acts 20:34–35), the Old Testament (1 Cor. 14:34), a few sayings of Christ (1 Cor. 7:10), and some general rules (1 Cor. 11:16), Paul is confident that his communities have the resources to mature. He is available if they need advice on certain matters (e.g., 1 Cor. 7:1; 1 Thess. 4:13) and occasionally visits them to see how they are doing (Acts 15:36). In a situation requiring discipline, he can still lay down the law, not, however, as an external, hierarchical authority as much as a significant fellow member whose spirit is present in their deliberations even when he is absent (1 Cor. 5:3–5; Col. 2:5). Even those with little status have the wisdom to deal with some disputes in the community (1 Cor. 6:4–5), though on other occasions the entire church should do so (1 Cor. 5:1–5). Paul's aim is to build up a community's ability to look after such matters, "working with" the members rather than "lording it over" them (2 Cor. 1:24). If he is forced to confront them, the "rod" that he brings is the rod of the Word (2 Cor. 10:3–6), and his preference is to come "in love and with a gentle spirit" (1 Cor. 4:21). His basic authority stems from the gospel he has been commissioned to preach, not by right from his apostolic commission. Only as long as his words reflect that gospel (Gal. 1:9) or are in accord with the Spirit (1 Cor. 7:40) should the churches give him a hearing. His authority is instrumental, not inherent, and, though powerful because of God's call, subject to his converts' Christian discernment.

The Roles of Paul's Colleagues in the Churches

Associates such as Timothy and Titus have only functional or derived authority based on the reputation of the work they have undertaken or on the task of transmitting Paul's message to the churches. They do not have an automatic right of entry. Often Paul has to argue their case, pointing out their involvement with him and knowledge of his affairs as well as their fidelity to the apostolic task, sometimes at risk to their own lives (1 Cor. 16:10–11; Phil. 2:19–23; Col. 4:7–8). When visiting churches, these colleagues have a role to play as itinerants (cf. 2 Cor. 7:15), not as residents. The pastoral letters are revealing here. Paul's associates do not have a settled and official role in the congregations but an ambassadorial and exemplary one. They do not reside among the congregations but only visit them for a defined period of time and exert spiritual rather than formal authority through the quality of their love and faithfulness to Paul's teaching (1 Tim. 2:12–15; 6:11–12; 2 Tim. 1:8; 2:22–24; 3:10; Titus 2:7). They are to relate to people in the churches in a familial way, reflecting their limited age and experience, rather than from a position of command (1 Tim. 5:1–2). They are to provide instruction for ordering certain aspects of worship and for governing the church rather than control and regulate the specifics of how church worship and government are conducted (1 Tim. 3:6; 2 Tim. 2:2–7; Titus 2:1–9). The key roles in the churches are for proven individuals and couples within their own ranks (1 Tim. 3:1–13; Titus 1:5–9). Paul's associates can only help identify these people through knowledge provided by the churches themselves.[2]

PAUL'S ROLE IN THE MISSION TEAM

Paul as a Collegial Leader

Paul's mission team was commissioned by a particular church, the church at Antioch, and at intervals reported back to it (Acts 13:1–3; 14:26–28). Yet it had a largely independent existence throughout the Mediterranean world. It always contained a number of core members who traveled much of the time with it but broke off now and again to fulfill a particular undertaking. It also contained a number of short-term members who came from various churches as the need or opportunity arose. Paul's team involved women and men, couples and singles, young and old, Greeks and Jews. It has been estimated that at times it contained up to forty members. Its prime tasks were to preach the gospel, plant churches among those who responded to it, and help network those churches and encourage them through occasional visits and letters. It was essentially a nonprofit organization engaged in mission activities.

The members of the group were drawn into the orbit of one person's ministry: Paul's. Paul is the one who is generally spoken of as "choosing," "sending," or "leaving" people and who generally decides, though with the agreement of his coworkers, what the next step in the work will entail (Acts 15:40; 16:1–3, 9; 18:1, 18–21; 19:21; 20:13, 16–17). Despite this, or rather because of Paul's understanding of his ministry as rooted in the gospel and embodied in Christ, Paul operates in a highly consultative and collegial way. He describes his staff as "coworkers" (Phil. 2:25) and as "brothers" (Acts 18:18) and regards them as having a ministry in their own right. They are not merely extensions of him and his work. This is clear from the way he names several of them separately at the beginning of many of his letters (as in 1 Cor. 1:1). His attitude is consistent with his hope that his fellow workers be welcomed and encouraged by the communities they visit (1 Cor. 16:10–11; 2 Cor. 8:22, 24; Phil. 2:20–22, 25–28; Col. 4:7, 12–13). Though there is a subordination to Paul, it is voluntary and personal rather than coercive and formal (1 Cor. 4:17; 2 Cor. 8:17).

Qualities That Mark Paul's Leadership

Underlying Paul's role are certain qualities that appear regularly in his writings. Among these, according to J. Oswald Sanders, are considerateness, courage, decisiveness, encouragement, faith, vision, modest self-appraisal, humility, the capacity to listen, magnanimity, patience, self-discipline, integrity, wisdom, zeal, and passion. Paul also displays an ability to handle conflict perceptively, criticism constructively, differences flexibly, finances scrupulously, time discerningly, and suffering redemptively. Through everything he demonstrates a commitment to regular communication with God, his colleagues, and groups influenced by his work. His leadership is based on a unique sense of calling by God, a dynamic awareness of identification with Christ, and an extraordinary versatility in the Spirit as he confronts diverse audiences, situations, and congregations.[3]

Historical Models of Leadership in the Church

The church in its many ecclesiastical expressions has a long and rich tradition of leadership expressed both inside its own community and in the world community at large. These distinct leadership approaches taken by various religious traditions may have relevant applications for leadership today.

The Benedictine Tradition

In the Benedictine Order, monks are viewed as preservers of tradition. Historically, they served as scribes who carefully copied manuscripts, thereby saving many treasures of classical antiquity during the so-called Dark Ages. Benedictine monasticism has flourished for more than fifteen hundred years in a variety of settings and in various cultures. Its fundamentals are contained in the Rule of St. Benedict, a formative document that has been influential in much communal development in the West to this day. As the leader of a monastery, the abbot is expected to hold together the creative tension between organizing and pastoring, between attending to the common good of all and the particular good of individuals. The role of the abbot is viewed as a kind of spiritual parent. In fulfilling this role, the abbot is expected to pass on wisdom (the sacred doctrine and tradition) as well as provide prudent guidance in a disciple's search for God. In addition, he is expected to understand the spiritual connection between administrative and pastoral duties.[4]

The temporal arrangements of a monastery are ordered to serve the spiritual good of the monks. Consequently, the abbot's spiritual leadership necessarily involves a concern for the practicalities of life. In this way, he is a steward of both the spiritual and the material resources of the monastery (Rule of St. Benedict 64). His stewardship expresses itself in delegating key tasks to others to direct the elements of the daily life of the community. The abbot is seen as a father (Rule 2:24) to those in the community. As a result, his leadership is viewed as fundamentally relational. The abbot is concerned for the good of the community and seeks the welfare of all its members. The abbot is also directed by the Order of St. Benedict to see himself as a physician (Rule 28). He must know how to "diagnose" the spiritual maladies of individual monks and the entire community, and he must know how to apply the right remedy. The Benedictine abbot is also seen as a teacher (Rule 2:11–15). Beyond his responsibility to teach monastic doctrine is his duty to teach a way of life. While he is to teach by word, he is also required to teach by the example of his life and actions. Though he is a guardian of tradition, the abbot must possess "a treasury of knowledge from which he can bring out what is old and new" (Rule 64:9).

In considering a monk for the office of abbot, a community must look for a person who demonstrates "wisdom in teaching" and "goodness of life" (Rule 64:2). The notion of wisdom carries with it the element of discretion. We might also call this prudence or discernment. The abbot must be able to size up the monks, taking note of their individual needs and gifts. He must know how to challenge the strong to greater advance in their spiritual journeys and also how to encourage the weak (Rule 64:17–18). The Rule goes on to encourage the abbot to include the community in key decisions, taking into account the thoughts of even the youngest members. In this way, discretion is used to make good participatory decisions.

The complex character of Benedictine leadership is best exhibited in the multiple roles the abbot undertakes simultaneously and seamlessly. Because he understands the long-term impact of his leadership on both his organization and his followers, like a parent or a guide, he exercises a combination of wisdom and care. Like a physician, the abbot serves as one who can identify and attend to the needs of his followers. Like a teacher, the abbot fulfills an instructional role through encouraging the personal and professional growth of his followers. He, like a manager, leads by exercising good and discreet stewardship of human and other resources. The abbot is comfortable delegating tasks while at the same time leading by example. These roles aptly capture the complexity of leadership required in today's world. Leaders must serve as guides, stewards, physicians, teachers, and empowerers, leading by example, displaying wisdom, and living lives of goodness.

The Lutheran Approach

Lutheran theology has always stressed God's complex work in the world, including his ability to affirm the goodness of created things and offices and the appropriateness of worldly vocations. Reason plays a central role, as does the application of common sense, in living life in the world.

The historical circumstances that gave birth to the Lutheran tradition provide a view of leadership as an act of reformation in the context of resistant systems. When Martin Luther is used as an exemplar of this approach to leadership, it expresses itself in three distinct tasks: (1) critique of the status quo or "defining reality," (2) constructive experimentation or risk taking, and (3) consolidation that has as its chief end continuity within the new order. This is a reformation model of change that requires courage, collaboration, and commitment and takes place within the context of Luther's conviction of the priesthood of all believers. This conviction enabled him to see every Christian as having full access to God, being able to express to others the full forgiveness of God, and exercising the divine right of sharing God's Word and reflecting God's Spirit.

What qualifies one for leadership from a Lutheran perspective? To begin with, one must understand the means of grace as it comes through the preached Word, baptism, the Lord's Supper, and the conversation and consolation of the community. Indeed, understanding one's baptism as a primary reminder of one's position as a child of God in the context of the commitment and fellowship of the faith community is highly relevant to understanding leadership. Doing so enables the believing person to live a life of security in the faith. As a leader, Luther constantly took himself back to the fundamental principles of the faith, to his security in baptism, and to his place in the community of faith. A leader is one who, like Luther, always keeps before him these key understandings.

This reformational understanding of leadership provides a model that is inward looking with respect to the person of the leader and outwardly focused on the tasks of leadership. A leader is one who with humility embraces his or her security in the faith, represented by baptism and confirmation of the benefits of living life within the faith community, namely, consolation, conversation, and communion. This inward confirmation of one's place in the world enables a leader to lead freely, intently, and openly. The Lutheran understanding of the priesthood of all believers helps leaders to view themselves less as overlords of their communities and more as representatives of them, exercising a role that belongs to every member even as it requires expression particularly in one.[5]

The Presbyterian Model

For Presbyterians, leadership is best portrayed by the classic Reformed understanding of the threefold office of Christ: prophet, priest, and king. In ancient Israel, these leadership functions were expressed separately by three people, and each was legitimate and necessary for carrying out God's will for the people. Prophets brought the message from God to the people, priests represented the needs of the people before God, and kings governed society according to God's will. In Presbyterian polity, these roles are expressed by ministers of the Word, who proclaim God's will to the church; deacons, who serve the felt needs of the people; and elders, who administer God's rule in the congregation.

In Christ, these three roles merge into one to create a complementary whole. As redeemer, Christ was at once prophet, priest, and king: He proclaimed the Word of God, exhibited mercy, and through his power healed the sick, forgave sins, and subdued the storm.[6] Since Christ encompasses all, it follows that in the Christian community those who profess Jesus as Lord should also seek to serve as prophet, priest, and king in a unified rather than a separate fashion. We can never again isolate the three offices; we must see them as a whole. This is not to say that a person must exhibit all three roles. Rather, all three must be represented in leadership.

The Presbyterian model offers significant insights for contemporary leadership. The priestly function reveals the need for empathy, a critical skill that has gained wide appeal in recent years. Empathy, often seen as a "soft" skill, has proven to be necessary for building relationships and understanding the perspectives of others. Effective communication is another key function of leadership and certainly ties in with the prophetic function. Leaders skilled at communicating a vision or a plan with clear, compelling, inspiring, and honest communication pave the way for enthusiastic implementation of their ideas. The ruling or kingly function is akin to the direction-setting ability of a leader. This is the ability to see the big picture.[7]

The Quaker Model

At the heart of the Quaker or Friends tradition is a rich belief in shared leadership. A designated or assigned individual leader is an alien concept. The Friends method of governance relies not on hierarchical structure to make decisions but rather on a "sense of the meeting" by the entire group. In this model of decision making, the emphasis is on the presence of Christ in the gathered community, and the practice of silence is used by all to discern the leading of the Spirit. Silence is not a vacuum or the absence of noise but a fullness, a space in which to hear the still, small voice of God. The gathered submit themselves to waiting on the Holy Spirit and to listening to one another in expectation that God's direction for the group will be revealed. Participants are expected to contribute their insights by speaking simply without repetition, rhetoric, or argumentativeness. Decisions are made through consensus rather than majority vote.[8]

The Quaker process of shared decision making is built on the fundamental belief that "all of us in this world are interdependent and must be responsible for each other."[9] No one is above anyone else, and the Spirit can speak through anyone in a Friends' meeting. Everyone has the responsibility to participate, whether orally or not, and each has the potential to offer insight. If one cannot improve on the silence, one does not speak. The spiritual power of group silence is recognized, and shared silence is a medium for group discovery and a way of sharing oneself with others and with God. Friends view silence as a highly accessible treasure. It is with silence that meetings begin and end, signaling dependence on the source of wisdom and giving time to open one's self to the workings of the Spirit.

This model invites organizational leaders to use their positional power to promote dialogue. The assigned leader is also a participant in seeking new solutions to pressing organizational issues. In the vulnerability of this approach, there is freedom for the assigned leader to contribute, listen, learn, and share his or her power. Quakerism opens up a way to better understand a style of shared leading and responsibility.[10]

The Pentecostal Movement

In the Pentecostal perspective, which has a much shorter but still influential history, an understanding of self emerges from an understanding of God as the giver of gifts and power. In this context, leadership is not viewed as a purely human characteristic. It is not a set of skills or knowledge that can be obtained or learned. Rather, leadership begins with understanding that one is a follower of Jesus and a vessel for the power of his Spirit. God is the chief leader who chooses human leaders. In this way, leadership is something that is derived from the sovereign operation of the God of the Bible. The greatness of human leadership is measured by how well the leader is a follower of God.

On the basis of Acts 2, Pentecostals believe that God pours out the gifts of the Spirit equally on all who earnestly seek the Spirit. They therefore view Christian leadership as transportable, adaptable, and personal. Within the Pentecostal movement, then, every member is a potential leader. All genuine leadership is based on spiritual power coming from the Spirit of God, and it emerges in the context of a loving community. Young people are encouraged to learn and publicly recite Scripture and express their gifts of the Spirit. Guidance and nurture are offered along with correction. In this environment, one emerges as a leader from within a context of mentoring and support.

According to the Pentecostal perspective, leadership can also be described as a spiritual calling, one that begins with being a good and faithful follower. A leader sees himself or herself as a vessel through which the power of God takes action to fulfill God's will on earth. Responding to the call is to take part in the present and future kingdom of God and enables the purposes of God to be accomplished in the here and now. Since any and all can be called, leadership is not for just a chosen few. It is open to all. From the Pentecostal perspective, therefore, leaders emerge from the community of faith in the context of support and encouragement, enabling the emergent leaders to grow and develop over time.[11]

IMPLICATIONS FOR LEADERSHIP IN DAILY LIFE

The approaches to leadership outlined above are not the only ones evident in Western societies. We could also explore the more military form of governance present in the Jesuit movement and the more representative character of Congregational church structure. These approaches and those outlined above have had an influence on the wider understanding of leadership in the West. In areas dominated by Catholicism and Anglicanism, this influence came through the close connection between church and state. On other occasions, as in some Protestant circles, it came through the gradual extension of church-based forms of leadership into civic and political structures as Christians began to realize that if they could govern their own religious affairs, they had the capacity to take on broader societal responsibilities. This happened in England, for example, in Presbyterian and Independent churches between the sixteenth and the eighteenth centuries.[12] Here and there even more radical Christian structures provided models of leadership that indirectly influenced the way leadership was understood and practiced. As yet, apart from documenting the influence of dissenting churches on the development of democratic forms of government between the Reformation and the Enlightenment, little research has been undertaken to demonstrate the specific connections between these traditions and wider social life.

These ecclesiastical traditions—in particular, the Benedictine, Lutheran, Presbyterian, Quaker, and Pentecostal traditions—offer rich and useful models of leadership applicable to today's organizations and groups.

While an abbot serves as the leader of a group of monks who share a common vision and values, he still needs to form the community and uphold and pass on the received tradition of the faith—its history, ethos, and fundamental values. His task is to form and re-form the community's basic identity and vision. The Benedictine abbot, then, must attend to the needs of the present, always with an eye to the future. The abbot is not only the preserver of the past but also the innovator of the future. Holding these two fundamental roles in tension is what makes the Benedictine abbot a unique leader.

Some important implications for leadership can be seen in the Lutheran approach. First, effective leadership carries with it a sense of calling, that is, one is led to lead. Second, leadership occurs within a shared community of followers and leaders; it is not an isolated activity. Third, foundational to good leading is knowing oneself, especially knowing oneself in God. This includes knowing one's strengths and weaknesses, embracing both success and failure, and keeping one's ego in check by remaining humble and grateful.

The priestly and prophetic dimensions of Christ's threefold office can be likened to the transforming kind of leadership articulated by James MacGregor Burns.[13] Such leadership seeks to create a dynamic and mutual relationship between leader and follower so that the morality and performance of both are raised. Each is transformed through the act of leading and following respectively. At the heart of the priestly functions of receiving confessions and serving as a mediator is empathy. As Hebrews 4:15 says, "For we do not have a high priest who is unable to sympathize with our weaknesses, but we have one who has been tempted in every way, just as we are—yet was without sin." Likewise, transforming leadership is an approach that includes and recognizes the importance of empathy, that is, the ability to momentarily suspend one's own needs for the sake of followers by putting oneself in their shoes to gain their perspective. The priestly function naturally leads to the prophetic function. Having employed empathy in the priestly function to understand more fully the perspective of followers, a leader then moves to the prophetic function and calls followers to higher ethical and moral levels, which is the keystone of transforming leadership. The kingly function corresponds with the governing and direction-setting dimensions of leadership. A leader establishes a plan and takes action with the goal of raising the level of motivation and morality among his or her followers. The quintessential example of this type of leadership is Mohandas Gandhi. He was a transforming leader who performed the roles of prophet, priest, and king for scores of followers.

The Quaker tradition offers a different perspective on leadership, one we might be tempted to call non-leadership, in the sense that all who participate in a Quaker meeting lead and follow simultaneously. Yet the model points to the importance of breaking down hierarchies and displaying trust and respect.

In addition, because all are involved in the decision-making process, there is a greater buy-in of all involved, which may in the long run save time at the implementation stage.

Pentecostals have traditionally had a difficult time knowing what kind of leadership to offer to the world Monday through Saturday. Because they believe that the kingdom of this world is in direct opposition to the kingdom of God, Pentecostals have traditionally opted not to get overly involved in the things of this world, including positions of leadership. At the same time, Pentecostals do bring to organizations a democratic approach to decision making by embracing the idea that each person should contribute to the final decision. Pentecostals take an emergent approach to leadership. In other words, they believe that the individual perceived to be the most influential, regardless of that person's title, will emerge as the leader of the group. These are valid approaches to leadership and fit well with organizations that are collaborative and less hierarchical.

The perspectives offered by these traditions provide rich insight into the multifaceted nature of leadership. Leadership can be viewed and understood from several vantage points, each of which is valid and necessary for a more thorough understanding of leadership. Each of these traditions has a unique view informed by its history, tenants, and key leaders. These ecclesiastical perspectives locate leadership in the context of faith convictions, and together they offer the core values of love, service, and high standards of ethical conduct.

These faith traditions reveal three common tensions that existed for leaders in the past and that are equally applicable to leaders today: the tension between (1) tradition and adaptation, (2) preservation and innovation, and (3) stability and change. These tensions represent critical questions leaders must face, such as, When may a leader seek a new adaptive approach to leading an organization, especially when the adaptation calls for abandoning tradition? At what point is it appropriate to leave behind important traditions? The watch phrase of this age is "innovate or die." Is there ever a time when it is better for a leader to call an organization to preservation rather than to innovation? And how does a leader hold together the duality of stability and change? Both must be in place for an organization and, most importantly, the people to function at their best. These are but a few of the timeless and essential questions these ecclesiastical traditions raise that help to deepen and expand an understanding of leadership.

Contemporary Studies of Leadership

In addition to examining the New Testament's normative approach to leadership and various historical models of leadership in the church, it is helpful to outline the contribution of academic studies of leadership during the last century and a half. These studies have examined past and present expressions of leadership and have sought to categorize, evaluate, and define their key elements in a way not attempted before.

During the latter half of the nineteenth century, reflection on leadership concentrated on the so-called great men theory. Study, therefore, focused on men who had affected the course of history in some way. Women did not receive much attention. The assumption was that great leaders emerged as the result of superior inherited capacities or particular circumstances of the time.

In the first half of the twentieth century, the focus moved to identifying traits characteristic of leaders. Various empirical research techniques were used in this undertaking. The hope was that identifying such traits would assist in the early detection of future leaders. In the late 1940s, however, a seminal article by Ralph Stogdill on personal factors in leadership reviewed the state of leadership studies and concluded that no consistent set of traits differentiated those who were leaders from those who were not.[14] Leadership depended on the relationships, situations, and culture in which leaders developed. Twenty-five years later, however, Stogdill analyzed the literature on leadership again, but this time he reserved a place for characteristics alongside the situational factors he had highlighted earlier.[15]

Since then, some researchers have focused on the centrality of traits in regard to people's perceptions of leadership, while other researchers have stressed the importance of only specific characteristics such as those related to the visionary and charismatic dimensions of leadership. Focusing on character traits would appear to correlate with popular perceptions in the media and among the public that leaders are special kinds of people. The traits that most consistently appeared on researchers' lists were intelligence, self-confidence, determination, integrity, and sociability. Certain others, such as masculinity and extroversion, appeared occasionally but not regularly. Meanwhile, subsequent research, as well as general observation, suggests that both hereditary and situational factors are at work in most examples of leadership. In addition, whether vision and charisma are necessary may be a function of the particular lifestage of an organization.

Throughout the 1950s and 1960s, attention in leadership studies moved from leadership traits to leadership activity, especially to leaders' behaviors and styles. Various studies conducted at Ohio State University and the University of Michigan distinguished between task-oriented and people-oriented approaches. The Managerial Grid later created by Robert Blake and Jane Mouton has been the most popular instrument for determining how managers do and should function.[16] It determines whether people are "impoverished" (low-people/low-results oriented), "country-club" (high-people/low-results oriented), "authority-compliant" (low-people/high-results oriented), "a team player" (high-people/high-results oriented), or "middle of the road" (between low- and high-people and low- and high-results oriented). This general approach to leadership provides a heuristic tool for understanding how leaders do or might function rather than offering a conceptual framework or detailed prescriptive advice. Research has not adequately shown how leaders' styles correlate with performance outcomes, nor has it validated the suggestion that high-people and high-results behavior is always the most effective.[17]

During the 1970s and 1980s, leadership studies paid increasing attention to the context in which leadership took place. A partial development in this direction was the contingency approach, which grew out of a modest critique of leadership style. Having analyzed the leadership styles of hundreds of leaders, especially military leaders, Fred Fiedler made empirically based generalizations about which styles were best suited to particular organizational contexts.[18] Fiedler believed that leaders tend to have a preferred style, whether oriented more to people or to results, and therefore the task is to find the best possible context that will produce the best from them. Fiedler's research indicated that a particular style could be correlated to certain combinations of situations and subordinates. He had to admit, however, that his research could not always explain why some people with a particular leadership style were more effective in some situations than in others or, when they were not, how to train organizations to adjust to the style of a leader. Because of the complexity of Fiedler's method—assessing style, situation, and power—it is a somewhat cumbersome approach to actual work situations.

A related approach that concentrated more fully on the context in which leadership took place was the more emphatic situational method favored by Paul Hersey, Kenneth Blanchard, and Dewey Johnson. Their widely used, regularly revised text *Management of Organizational Behavior: Utilizing Human Resources* emphasizes the task- and people-oriented, or directive and supportive, dimensions of leadership, but it stresses that each has to be applied in a given situation.[19] This means there is no one ideal leadership style and opens up the possibility of leaders diagnosing and then adapting their approach to fit their circumstances. Hersey and Blanchard are more confident than Fiedler in a leader's capacity to adjust his or her leadership to the commitment and competence of subordinates. They see a flow from a delegating, to a supporting, to a directing, to a coaching style. This approach has not as yet been subject to verification by many empirical studies, and the notion of commitment on the part of subordinates is vaguely defined and correlated with competence. The flow of leadership styles developed by Hersey and Blanchard also seems to fit some situations better than others, depending on the maturity of those in junior positions, and works best with relatively homogeneous groups of subordinates.

Building on the recognition that the dynamics of leader-follower relationships are central to the exercise of leadership, James MacGregor Burns fully developed the transforming leadership approach.[20] Burns distinguished between transactional leadership and transforming leadership. The first focuses on what leaders and followers gain in exchange for cooperating. This is well exemplified in election campaigns and voting day. Transforming leadership, on the other hand, seeks to raise the level of motivation and morality among both leaders and followers. Alan Bryman and others emphasized the role of charisma in this, virtually in character trait terms.[21] A few years later, Bernard Bass formulated a more sophisticated model of transformational leadership.[22] He argued that transactional and transforming leadership were not opposites but on a continuum. He also suggested that while the presence of charisma may be a factor in leadership, it is not in itself sufficient for its effective exercise.

An empirical edge was given to Bass's work through the results of extensive interviews with leaders conducted by and incorporated in the work of Warren Bennis and Burt Nanus,[23] who have been influential in spreading the transformational approach to leadership.[24] The basic ingredients of leadership emphasized by Bass were idealized influence (or charisma), inspirational motivation, intellectual stimulation, and individualized consideration. For Bennis, they were guiding vision, passion, integrity, trust, curiosity, and daring. The key skills identified by Nanus were farsightedness, guiding change, organization design, anticipatory learning, initiative, confident independence, and integrity.

Bennis and Nanus built on but criticized the transactional or exchange theory, according to which followers give leaders their allegiance and effort in return for rewards, as only partly adequate. They argued that the theory failed to understand the wider dynamics between these two groups. It also settled for a leader's willingness to work within the rules, values, culture, and constraints of a situation rather than seeking to change them. The work of Allan Cohen and David Bradford, *Influence without Authority,* suggests that the highest form of influence on others moves through and beyond exchange to partnering between leader and followers.[25] Wilfred Drath and Charles Palus refined this by suggesting that instead of starting with the relationship between a leader and others, one should start with the work group or organization of people who together seek to make their work meaningful and transformational, out of which leaders and leadership comes.[26] Despite its significant value, transformational leadership is based primarily on an orientation to highly visible leaders and suffers from a lack of conceptual clarity. Many, therefore, regard it as less a full-scale theory of leadership than one that augments or refines other approaches.

Over the last two decades, people have developed more complex theories as to how leadership operates and develops. In doing so, they have taken into account a wider array of situational, relational, and cultural factors; how people exercise leadership through organizational structures as well as personal interactions; the place of personal and organizational values and the responsibility of organizations to their communities and society; and the values of individual leaders, which has pushed the importance of ethical codes and ethical decision making to the fore. They have also recognized the increasing multicultural and global character of internal and external organizational life respectively and have paid more attention to the workings of other cultures and how to work effectively with them. Initial interest is also being shown in the influence of religious, including Christian, perspectives on leadership, particularly on the various tensions such perspectives create. Seven key tensions relate to God and mammon, love and competition, people needs and profit obligations, family and work, humility and success, charity and wealth, faithfulness and tolerance.[27]

Accompanying ongoing research into leadership is popular writing on the subject. Such writing is oriented more to practitioners and action than to educationalists and analysis. Some of these writers, such as Warren Bennis and Burt Nanus, are extremely popular. Others include Peter Block, Stephen Covey, Max De Pree, John Gardner, James Kouzes, Barry Posner, and Margaret Wheatley. Whatever their differences, these writers tend to share a number of common emphases:

- They frequently define leadership as a potential in everyone, not just a special group.
- They see authority as shared, distributed, or pervasive throughout an organization.
- They emphasize the servant-leader paradigm or the image of the leader as a steward or trustee.
- They use the language of organizational purpose and vision rather than positional power.
- They focus on transformational language, attitudes, and practices.
- They believe leaders model the way and are prime encouragers of others.
- They see leaders as key figures on a team rather than as soloists.
- They see a reciprocal relationship with and the empowerment of followers as vital themes.
- They emphasize the importance not only of ethics but also of wider values in relation to leadership.

Some of these emphases have much in common with biblical perspectives on leadership. This should be encouraging to those developing and practicing a Christian perspective.

Conclusion

Paul's approach to leading and the various ecclesiastical traditions of leadership discussed in this chapter provide a glimpse into some important ways of understanding Christian leading. These models reveal certain themes that can serve as a guide for a person of faith who wishes to be intentional about integrating faith into leadership.

The themes seem to take the form of metaphors that can help us better understand the many facets of leadership discussed in this chapter. A metaphor is a powerful tool that sheds light on complex ideas or issues and opens up new perspectives. The power of a metaphor lies in its ability to take knowledge about one thing and apply it to something less known. A metaphor bridges the gap between familiarity and unfamiliarity. By comparing dissimilar things, we can comprehend the unfamiliar in familiar terms.[28] This increases insight and depth of understanding. In this case, it increases insight into leadership and how it can be expressed from a Christian perspective.

For instance, Paul suggested that leadership in the church resembles family life—mother and child, father and child, and child and parent. This metaphor for leadership stresses the affectionate relationship involved in leadership and the responsibility leaders have of leading people toward a deeper understanding of God and his love for each individual.

Likewise, the Benedictine tradition illuminates the role of the abbot using the metaphors of parent, physician, teacher, and steward. A leader of faith must lead like a parent who guides, like a physician who heals, like a teacher who facilitates learning, and like a steward who exercises good judgment over resources.

The leader as reformer is an excellent metaphor from the Lutheran tradition. It underscores the fact that leaders must challenge static and confining ways of doing things and reform them into life-giving processes that can be self-directed. This creates greater freedom and personal responsibility.

Leadership can also be described using the metaphors of prophet, priest, and king—the threefold office of Christ from the Presbyterian perspective. As discussed above, the prophet proclaims, the priest reconciles, and the king rules or administers.

But leadership is not only about proclamation. It is also about listening, as the Quaker tradition reveals using the metaphor of silence. Leadership is like silence, not an empty space but a holding space where what is important and necessary can be heard.

Leadership is also like a vessel waiting to be filled with God's Spirit and empowered to do good works, as the Pentecostal tradition suggests. Leadership is like a gift received, and this gift comes with power to do good work in the name of Jesus. To receive this gift, the Pentecostals remind us, one must first be a good follower, open and receptive, willing to respond and to be led.

This chapter is rich in metaphors that shed light on the practice of faithful leading. When leaders discover ways to integrate their faith into their leadership, the organizations they lead and the people in them experience clarity of purpose, an increased desire to serve, and renewed energy.

The development of an understanding of leadership and the way certain studies influenced trends in leadership shed further light on leadership. From this discussion we see that leadership involves at least four important elements: (1) the person of the leader, (2) the relationship between leader and follower, (3) the task a leader is attempting to accomplish, and (4) the influence of the context or setting in which a leader leads.

In keeping with a metaphor approach, these elements are like concentric circles, like ripples in a pond. The person of the leader is the inner-most circle. Next is the leader-follower relationship, then the task, and lastly the setting of leadership. Each is important and necessary for a complete picture of leadership. This metaphor captures the dynamic energy of leadership. Leadership has the power to affect people, projects, and contexts in significant and powerful ways. This reveals the importance of leading from wholeness and from a clear sense of who one is in God, because the substance of a leader will move to each concentric circle and will touch each element with light or with darkness, causing good or ill depending on the character of the leader.

Metaphors are helpful in describing the attributes of leadership and even offer insight into what a leader actually does. But more is needed. Therefore, it is necessary to move a step beyond metaphor to ask, What actions should a faithful leader take to lead in ways consistent with his or her faith? In general, leadership that bears the imprint of faith includes the following characteristics:

- intentionality: Leadership requires intentional action, and faith compels action toward spiritual integrity and ethical consistency.
- reflection: This discipline leads to spiritual depth, greater self-knowledge, and organizational insight.
- self-evaluation: Leaders who incorporate their faith ask, "Is the person I see in the mirror the person I say I am and want to be?" Leading from faith involves a willingness to receive feedback and to correct course when necessary.
- covenant building: Faithful leaders build alliances, create communities, seek partnerships, and promote teamwork.
- intellectual integrity: This involves seeing the world as it is, not as one wants it to be. Such leaders never stop increasing their knowledge about human nature and the world.
- ethical integrity: Upholding moral and ethical values in decision making, actions, and communication is one of the hallmarks of faithful leading.
- followership: Leadership is never devoid of good followership. The faithful leader is a servant first, and from that emerges the desire to lead.
- perpetual learning and development: Leadership is never mastered; it requires constant learning and development. Leaders of faith recognize that their role as a servant to an organization requires them to constantly hone their leadership talent.

These are some of the key benchmarks for faith-filled leading. A leader of faith will find in these commitments the joy of service, the integrity of faith, and the fruitful results of honoring God through their leadership.

The next chapter further examines the contemporary discussion of leadership, focusing on leadership approaches that contain a spiritual dimension.

the emerging spiritual and religious dimensions of leadership

As the discussion of contemporary studies of leadership in the last chapter intimated, until recently there was little interest in the spiritual dimension of leadership. This dimension was bracketed out by the largely value-free approach that dominated studies in many fields from the late nineteenth century through much of the twentieth century. Consideration of the ethical dimension of leadership was also affected by this approach. Over the last few decades, however, the growing interest in the spiritual dimension of life has opened up discussion of it in relation to work and leadership.

This chapter looks first at implicit indications of this growing interest (Stephen Covey serves as a case study), then at writings and people in which the spiritual dimension of leadership appears more overtly (Václav Havel is a prime example), and finally at two basic Christian approaches to leadership (offered by Patricia Brown and Max De Pree). As well as demonstrating the growing recognition that spirituality is integral to leadership, this chapter opens the door to a more detailed examination of faith-based approaches to leadership.

Implicit Signs of Spiritual Concerns

Writings on work and leadership by some well-known writers who do not expressly associate themselves with a religious perspective nonetheless contain interesting echoes of spiritual concerns.

The English management specialist and ethicist Stephen Pattison has argued provocatively that much so-called secular thinking and writing about management displays a form of utopian religious faith.[1] He has since focused his argument more specifically on approaches to leadership.[2]

He begins by stating that ideas about leadership, though rarely linked specifically with faith, are often supported by assumptions and beliefs that spring from a particular worldview and that these are permeated by quasi-religious and at times religious factors. These factors affect both the content of such ideas as well as the force with which they are held and communicated. Pattison's aim is to "illuminate the unrecognized beliefs and practices that are often found in leadership, whether in the public sector or the private sector."[3] His analysis of several leading writers on leadership falls into four sections.

First, Pattison argues that many theorists and consultants are primarily selling "faith, hope, and meaning" as much as specific knowledge or techniques. These religious-sounding possibilities are offered on the basis of such beliefs as:

- Human beings have the capacity to control the world and shape the future.
- Clear goals and objectives for the future are attainable.
- The customer's wants and immediate gratification are ultimate or sovereign.
- Everything significant can be measured objectively.
- The success of an organization is the greatest good.

In his view, these beliefs, expressing attitudes derived from the Enlightenment and the Industrial Revolution, are inadequate from a Christian point of view.

Second, Pattison focuses on the presence of mystical metaphors in many writings on leadership. Since language is the main tool leaders use to exercise influence, their choice of words vividly displays what is most basic and important to them. Imagery, especially key and recurring metaphors, plays a powerful role in understanding and communicating. In leadership literature, many such metaphors have a religious resonance. Among these are:

- vision: This describes what an organization would like to be and therefore provides a powerful motivation for those who belong to it.
- mission: This is often encapsulated in a mission statement and inspires commitment to an organization and its goals.

Such metaphors have their roots in and carry unconscious connotations of the language of religious contemplation and vocation. Other terms that are often used as a kind of mantra in connection with leadership, such as servant or service, also fit in this category.

Third, Pattison analyzes sacramental rituals. Most organizations develop customary ways of doing things that assume such symbolic importance that they are taken for granted. They are seen as the only proper means of tackling certain objectives, even though they do not have the instrumental function people assume they have and often fail to deliver the goods. Pattison does not say there is something substantively religious about these activities but that functionally they operate in a way similar to religious rituals. His main examples are:

- Strategic planning promises much but is often irrelevant the moment it is completed. There are too many variables to take into account, and people cannot keep pace with changing circumstances.
- The bottom line is a form of calculation that ultimately determines what happens and is regarded as unquestionable and inviolable.
- Preoccupation with the processes for exercising leadership can become a kind of fetish with which people are obsessed.

Fourth, Pattison notes the following parallels between assumptions and behavior in the business world and in some evangelical, especially sectarian, Christian groups. Among his examples are:

- Corporate identity is prized and requires loyal adherence.
- People are converted to the organization's aims, values, and practices.
- A sense of purpose and community comes through belonging to the organization.
- The search for excellence and striving for improvement of quality are forms of perfectionism.
- Values of obedience and conformity are affirmed despite rhetoric of individual empowerment.

The exercise of leadership itself, he argues, is sometimes replete with religious echoes. For example, some analysts of leadership emphasize charismatic authority and personal giftedness rather than professional knowledge and competence. This is a feature of many traveling evangelists of leadership, such as Tom Peters and others, who regularly hit the corporate sawdust trail with their messages of organizational salvation, renewal, and growth. These speakers and writers also stress the need for personal asceticism in leaders as a result of the hours they are expected to work and familial responsibilities and other close relationships they are expected to forgo.

Pattison concludes:

> Belief or faith free leadership is probably not realistic or even desirable. . . . [Leadership] contains important symbolic, non-rational, and even spiritual elements. It is easy to deny them, but instead . . . leaders might become more critically aware of their basic beliefs and assumptions. This awareness would allow them to engage in more careful assessment of the nature, content, effects, and desirability of their beliefs. In this way, it would become possible for [them] to possess their faith systems more clearly than [to be] possessed by them.[4]

In the next chapter, we take this idea a step further and evaluate explicitly religious approaches to and practices of leadership and propose ways of understanding and exercising leadership that are consonant with a Christian perspective. We turn now, however, to consider the writings of an influential communicator on leadership whose work provides an example of implicit religious ideas.

A CASE STUDY: STEPHEN COVEY

Stephen Covey's *Seven Habits of Highly Effective People* has been one of the most widely read books since the late 1980s.[5] Within a decade it had sold over ten million copies and been translated into twenty-eight languages. It was followed two years later by his *Principle-Centered Leadership,*[6] which he has since followed with two cowritten books on personal and family development.

There are several reasons for Covey's popularity. His books combine several strands, each of which is appealing in its own right. These include elements of popular management theory, fashionable morality, pseudo-science, universal spirituality, and technique. They appear to strike a chord with those in middle-level bureaucratic positions in larger organizations who experience a lack of power and purpose in their work and are willing to swim in some of the prevailing currents of contemporary morality. For them, he provides a kind of "catechism" made up of formularized wisdom, spiritual resonance, and simplified management theory. The first of these, as one of the appendixes to a recent book shows, draws on Egyptian, Greek, Chinese, Indian, and Hebrew wisdom literature.[7] The second speaks to the lack of and the search for a spiritual dimension in the workplace and in the exercise of leadership.

Covey is a committed, lifelong Mormon who taught business management and organizational behavior for twenty years at Brigham Young University before becoming head of a large consulting firm and a well-known writer. In his books, however, he does not talk about his religious views. He speaks of God only in a generic way and refuses to acknowledge the particularly Mormon character of his approach. In his important article "White Magic: Capitalism, Mormonism, and the Doctrines of Stephen Covey," Alan Wolfe suggests that part of the reason for this is Mormonism's long-standing decision, going back to its founder Joseph

Smith,[8] to suppress some of its views so as not to alienate the wider American public. It is also partly due to Covey's desire to appeal to the mainline culture of the United States as well as to a worldwide audience. Despite Covey's statements to the effect that the core principles and habits he identifies are those everyone knows to be true, Wolfe argues persuasively that the Mormon influences in Covey's work are incontrovertible. Wolfe does not argue that Covey's works contain a simple translation of Mormon beliefs, values, and practices into managerial language. What we find in them, he says, is a set of assumptions that, whatever their other influences and associations, have identifiable Mormon roots.

First, Covey conveys a faith in people's capacity to know and do what he prescribes. This faith in others is essentially the only kind Covey mentions. Unlike both Protestants and Catholics, Covey believes in the essential goodness of human nature. For example, Adam did not sin. He simply exercised his power of choice to eat from the tree of knowledge. This is why he could become God's son and even a divine being. He does acknowledge the presence of "bad habits" stemming from such forces as the appetites, pride, and ambition. Though he describes them as "character issues," he does not doubt the human ability to deal with them.

According to Covey, "natural laws" are intrinsic to every civilized society, just as physical laws are part of the fabric of the entire creation. Since, from a Mormon point of view, human beings were present in the beginning with God, it is not surprising that these ways of operating were built into human beings. At their best, people know them and operate by them. It is only because humans do not do so consistently that these ways of operating need to be transformed into habits that are automatically practiced. The notion of obedience to law is in accord with the central place of law in Mormon thinking and behavior.

Covey's seven principles are as follows: (1) be proactive; (2) begin with the end in mind; (3) put first things first; (4) think win-win; (5) seek understanding before being understood; (6) synergize; and (7) self-renew regularly.[9] Although Covey uses the language of truth in talking about these principles, they are more procedural than conceptual or moral in character. According to Covey, principle-centered leaders are characterized by the following: They 1) continually learn; (2) have a service orientation; (3) radiate positive energy; (4) believe in other people; (5) lead a balanced life; (6) see life as an adventure; (7) possess synergy; and (8) engage in holistic self-renewal.[10] The last two of these are identical with his last two principles. The remainder contain a mixture of attitudinal, educational, and lifestyle elements that touch on character but do not deeply explore it.

Though Covey uses the language of "moral compassing," he distinguishes between values, principles, and practices, arguing that the former are too general and the latter too specific. His seven principles primarily form a kind of procedural manual. As such, they have more in common with a daily ritual than a moral code. Covey's First Things First, a manual of "daily reflections," is consonant with this. Though he uses, indeed highlights, the language of habits, these too have only a secondary, at times marginal, reference to developing character. They relate more to aspects of self-development and lifestyle.

Covey's belief that anyone who so desires can put these principles into practice correlates with the Mormon view that human beings have the necessary free will and willpower to fulfill their divine responsibilities. People are able to understand the principles embedded within them and to turn them into habits that influence behavior. The power of choice is a recurring theme in Covey's writings, and basic needs incline people to make positive use of this. Though resolve and willpower are not always enough, contractual arrangements with others with similar goals can help people do what is required. Accordingly, there is no need of grace to assist people or of the Spirit to empower them, doctrines that have little place within a Mormon framework. Though he sometimes talks about the importance of the "character ethic"—mainly in opposition to the "personality ethic"—the central elements of character are inadequately defined. Integrity, for example, is described as merely the value people place on themselves, and maturity is merely the balance people need to strike between courage and consideration. Love rates a brief mention, but Covey offers little texture and depth regarding what it involves.

When differences arise, tolerant and nonjudgmental attitudes should govern relationships between people. For Covey, the Golden Rule, or the Law of Reciprocity, as he calls it, is basic. Covey is influenced here by Mormonism's weak understanding of sin and atonement. As a result, there is little that is demanding, costly, and sacrificial in his view of relationships. Though he recognizes the need for people to move from accepting individual responsibility for their actions to developing interdependence with others, this is cast in terms of solidarity rather than genuine community.

In essence, then, as Wolfe says, "Mormonism's great contribution to the work of Stephen Covey has been to provide the unwritten assumptions for a secular version of what life means in organizations in which most people spend most of the time spinning their wheels."[11] The mixture of religious elements in Covey's writings—some genuinely spiritual ones springing from Mormonism's debt to its Jewish and Christian antecedents, and some more expressive of the natural religious instincts of the human heart—appeal to a wide range of people who have either lost touch with their religious heritage, do not know how to connect it to the life of work, or crave something they have lost in their adoption of more secular attitudes. It is precisely the "hidden presence" of this religious mixture that has proven so popular and successful.

Explicit Discussions of Spirituality in the Workplace

While some writers have incorporated hints of spiritual concerns into their writings, others have engaged in a more explicit discussion of spirituality and work. Of these, some have conducted specialized explorations of the link between spirituality and leadership. In these writings, the term *spirituality* has three basic meanings. All three sometimes appear in a single collection,[12] but individual authors usually tend to favor one over the others.

A Definition of Spirituality

Some writers define spirituality in humanistic terms: It has the capability—generally ascribed to the inner person or being, soul or spirit—to enable people to transcend their normal selves or to give expression to the multiplicity of selves within them. This approach draws on various traditions that speak about the soul, treating them basically as myths from which can be drawn important lessons for being and doing.[13] This view of spirituality rejects any religious connotations associated with the word, meaning any connection with the beliefs of an established faith.

Other writers define spirituality in more cosmic or interreligious terms, as the presence of some form of higher power or divinity that permeates all life and nature and into which people can tap to find resources for living and working.[14] Though this approach also avoids giving spirituality a traditional religious significance, it draws from a wide range of ancient traditions, especially Eastern, and forms of New Age spirituality.

What is interesting, however, is the way a number of key Greek terms from the New Testament have been increasingly drawn into the discussion of spirituality and the workplace. Alongside more common Judeo-Christian words such as *love, care, stewardship,* and *trust,* terms such as *koinōnia* (working in partnership toward a common end), *diakonia* (humble service in a significant cause), and *metanoia* (a radical change of mind and heart) now also appear in the literature.

Spirituality and Leadership

In a growing number of writings on leadership in particular, the same three approaches to spirituality appear. A mainly humanistic understanding is present in Lee Bolman and Terrence Deal's *Leading with Soul: An Uncommon Journey of Spirit.*[15] Though the authors draw on a diverse mixture of spiritual traditions, they also utilize philosophy, the social sciences, and poetry. They include certain extraordinary, not supernatural, aspects of spirituality but focus mainly on the human "spiritual center."

Russ Moxley provides a more developed approach along these lines in *Leadership and Spirit: Breathing New Vitality and Energy into Individuals and Organizations.*[16] Moxley, influenced by the writings of Parker Palmer, talks about how dispirited many workers are today, the fact that leadership often suffocates spirit, and the need for leadership that is not only inspiring but also inspiriting. His solution is that "we must learn to be our true selves and our whole selves," from which proceed new ways of doing leadership.[17] For Moxley, spirit is the life force that weaves through and permeates all experiences, defining a person's unique self and drawing him or her toward inner wholeness. It also connects people to everything that exists and draws them into communion with everyone with whom they come in contact. Spirit is "other" than whom people normally are. It is to be uncovered rather than discovered, appropriated rather than developed. Spirit is something prior to and different from a particular expression of religion. While religion can be a pathway to it or can complement it, spirit is in essence simply "being fully human."[18]

Though intangible, spirit is as real as anything else. People encounter it in the midst of the ordinary and the everyday as well as through the extraordinary and the mystical. People sense it in busyness and activity as well as in solitude and touch it in moments of apparently random events as much as in unexpected synchronicities. The experience of spirit within comes in times of renewal, integration, and vitality. The experience of spirit between people occurs in moments of honoring others, treating them as ends rather than as means, and going beyond contractual or instrumental to covenantal or communal relationships. The experience of spirit in organizations happens through such specific practices as joint stock ownership, distributed leadership, and shared vision. Leadership that embodies and releases the spirit goes beyond being individualistic and coercive. It stresses partnership and balance of power, knowing and embracing one's full self as well as affirming one's interdependence. It also recognizes the importance of calling and gifts, authenticity and wholeness. It nurtures itself through the inner disciplines of silence, meditation, and journaling and through the outer disciplines of deep listening and sharing life stories, personal growth workshops, and learning through work itself.

A wider understanding that gives a more transcendent sense to spirit is found in a collection by Peter Vaill called *Spirited Leading and Learning: Process Wisdom for a New Age,*[19] which contains connections with the process philosophy of Charles Hartshorne in his *Reality as Social Process.*[20] For Vaill, contrary to much thinking and training, "managerial leadership is not a secular enterprise. . . . It forces us to rethink the boundary between the secular and the sacred, between the natural and the transcendental."[21] Starting at the opposite end from Moxley, he first discusses the essential spirituality of organizations rather than of persons. Organizations are not secular entities, nor does their spiritual basis lie only in certain religiously minded individuals. Organizations possess an inherent divine foundation. Though recent decades have witnessed a widespread loss of meaning in organizations, they have an inherent coherence that enables their members to find meaning and credibility. This arises from more than leadership stability and institutional traditions—both of which are now in short supply—or from vision and mission statements.

In this way, Vaill opens up the possibility of organizations having a spiritual grounding that is located in the search for meaning. To do justice to this, people need "to search beyond what they can do *to* and/or *on* and/or *within* oneself,"[22] for it is the self itself that is inadequate. Only a turn to a transcendent source of meaning will open up people and organizations to greater possibilities. This is an ongoing process that amounts to "learning to think and communicate theologically—something, unfortunately, that is not presently contemplated by any known MBA program."[23] What makes this search more difficult is the fundamental dislocation today between spirituality and everyday life. Yet unless spiritual life takes place within organizations, genuine life will not take place. Pursuing the spiritual life at a purely personal level within an organization is insufficient, though unfortunately, organizations that consciously set out to be more spiritual do not always succeed. Still, people do experience moments of quality work, loving teamwork, extraordinary leadership, united focus, and self-transformation in the workplace, all of which point to the existence of a spiritual dimension.

This is even more the case when an organization values such experiences. They can do so at the economic, technical, communal, adaptive, and transcendent or meaning-creating levels. Spiritual life is not restricted to the last of these but can be experienced in and through any of them. For example, at the economic level, spiritual awareness may be concerned with the meaning of waste, loss, ill-gotten gains, and windfalls. At the technical level, spirituality may involve notions of respect for materials, craft, and quality. At the communal level, it may revolve around a sense of genuine fellowship. At the adaptive level, it may concern forbearance and forgiveness. At the transcendent level, it may assist the discovery of meaning itself, and finding the best language for it, to which others can orient their lives.

While a spiritual dimension to life is available to everyone in an organization, whether they have specific religious faith or not, it makes more sense to those who have faith in some kind of divinity. It is especially important for those at the executive level. Indeed, "to a large extent executive development for leadership in modern organizations is spiritual development."[24] We should therefore ask, "What are the implications for the spiritual condition and the spiritual growth of individual executives, and the need for them to foster vision, vitality, and spirit in the organizations they lead?"[25] For Vaill, executive formation must go beyond talking about the vision and mission of purposeful thinking and acting, for these deal with only externals. They do not take into account the personal qualities, core values, and deep passions that generate vision and mission. Such matters, particularly feelings, are too often suppressed or ignored in the intellectually oriented training and operation of leaders. Only by encouraging people to engage in spiritual development will the necessary qualities, values, and feelings come into play. This development involves: (1) embracing new perspectives and the possibilities they open up; (2) exhibiting a passionate reason and faith; (3) developing an open value system with creative boundary management; (4) building a fellowship of kindred organizational spirits; (5) forging a new spiritual vocabulary and grammar that rehabilitate old theological terms, especially through conscious prayer; (6) appreciating the spirit in increasingly larger wholes; and (7) enhancing the ability to center one's attention and energies in the present, where spirit is mainly found. This entire area of spirituality, Vaill contends, raises "the most important contemporary problems in management."[26]

We turn from this survey of spirituality in the workplace in general and in leadership in particular to a case study of explicit spirituality at work in the life of an international leader.

A Case Study: Václav Havel

Václav Havel is an example of a figure who has connected spirituality with leadership. He possesses a profound religious faith that, while not Christian in nature, includes many elements derived from or similar to those of Christianity, so much so that a leading Christian apologist devoted a book to him and encouraged his readers to view Havel as an exemplary role model of leadership at work.[27] After becoming a well-known figure in the artistic world of Prague, and as a result of his involvement in public demonstrations against the communist regime, Havel unexpectedly found himself thrust into the political limelight. In 1990, he became president of Czechoslovakia and, in 1992, after the country's division, of the Czech Republic, a position he holds to this day.

Born in 1936 to middle-class parents, Havel experienced both Nazi and communist rule. When he was twelve years old, his parents' property was confiscated by the state, and the family was forced to move to a hamlet where there was little employment and poor accommodations. In his mid teens, after completing elementary school, he went to work as a laboratory assistant and attended night school in the city. Five years later he enrolled in a university, but his studies were interrupted by two years of military service. In his early twenties, he developed an interest in drama and, with others, founded a regimental theater company.

In 1960, he started work at a theater in Prague, first as a stagehand and finally as a dramatist, remaining there for eight years. During that time, he joined the Writer's Union and sought to hold its members accountable for their role in society. Yet "the last thing the young Havel wanted to be was a leader. His heroes were playwrights whose genre was the theater of the absurd. Writers of this kind of drama do not take it upon themselves to change society."[28] His plays did not present heroes on whom people could project their hopes for action but rather encouraged them to face and do something about their personal and social misery. In Havel's view, the only real solutions are those people discover within and for themselves. "Theater does not mediate that kind of help—it is not a church. Theater ought to be—with God's help—theater."[29]

In 1968, Havel became caught up in the dramatic events of the so-called Prague Spring, when the nation briefly sought to create what the world press called "the human face of socialism." He gradually got involved in debates, meetings, and declarations. After the Soviet tanks moved in, he focused again on his work in the theater, but within three years, he found himself publicly branded as an enemy of the state and (unsuccessfully) indicted for subversion. He withdrew, as he says, into a kind of "internal exile." Then in April 1975, he wrote a letter to the country's leader, Gustav Husak, describing the desolate state of the country and the entropic state of the government. Though his letter was widely distributed by the underground, for him it was more an exercise in "auto therapy" than a thoughtful protest.[30] A short time later, he played a key role in organizing a well-orchestrated campaign to defend a group of musicians placed on trial for performing seditious songs.

In the late 1970s, he was heavily involved in the production of Charter 77, a human rights petition that sprang from an emerging network of people and organizations committed to social and political change. Because he was the youngest of its spokesmen and also extremely mobile because he owned a car, the authorities (wrongly) identified him as the key person behind it. He was arrested and held for eighteen months, released after being publicly disgraced, and then, after a brief period, imprisoned for an additional three years. It was only when he became seriously ill that he was released, though the authorities were also facing increasing international pressure to do so.

During his imprisonment, the spiritual dimension of his life found expression in letters he wrote to his wife. It was stimulated by a strong, mystical experience of standing "at the edge of the finite" and glimpsing transcendent "Being." This cast "a deep and obvious meaning" over his life, flooded him with a sense of "ultimate happiness and harmony," and resulted in his being "somehow struck by love."[31] Though Havel, for fear of over-objectifying the divine, often hesitates to call this Being "God," his definition "seems identical to a fully theistic God. All the characteristics are there, including personality."[32] This personal Being longs for all persons to be reintegrated with one another and with the divine. However "abstract and vague" such talk may sound, for Havel, it signifies a "vivid, intimate, and particular" relationship.[33] He had a sense that "in everything I do I touch eternity in a strange way." Though there were rumors of his conversion to Catholicism in prison, he responded that a full, inward acceptance of "Christ as the son of God" was a step he had not yet taken.[34]

In the years that followed, he did not see himself as a leader of the struggle for change but as someone who had a gift for words and organization. His involvement was simply an extension of his work as an artist. As Havel explained in the 1980s:

I've never taken a systematic interest in politics, political science, or economics; I've never had a clear-cut political position, much less expressed it in public. I'm a writer, and I've always understood my mission to speak the truth about the world I live in, to bear witness to its terrors and its miseries—in other words, to warn rather than hand out prescriptions for change. Suggesting something better and putting it into practice is a politician's job, and I've never been a politician and never wanted to be. . . . It is true that I've always been interested in politics, but only as an observer and a critic, not as someone who actually does it.[35]

The only kind of politics that attracted him was one from below, arising from everyday life and operating in a grassroots way. His general interest in public life sprang from a spiritual conviction that the world is "going through a great departure from God that has no parallel in history" and that it is only through a disavowal of this atheistic foundation and a spiritual renewal involving a "global revolution in human consciousness" that a new world of meaning, values, and community can be built.[36] This explains the importance Havel attaches to people's changing self-awareness, personal liberation, and social consciousness, to their growing hunger for truth, capacity to act more freely, and willingness to take greater risks. If people do not take this lead, official forms of leadership for change are either impossible or unproductive.

On the other hand, he did not see himself purely as a playwright. As he once said, "Though I have a presence in many places, I don't really have a firm, predestined place anywhere, in terms of neither my employment, nor my expertise, nor my education and upbringing, nor my qualities and skills."[37] He always felt something of an amateur in the various arenas in which he operated. He was certainly one of the most effective and respected participants in the events of 1989, especially in the formation of the Civic Forum, the first legal opposition in Czechoslovakia in forty years. As a result, after the fall of the communist government, he was approached about becoming president. This prospect took him by surprise. He did not feel naturally qualified or gifted for such a position. He had no formal political or bureaucratic experience. His arena was the world of culture and grassroots action, not public life and policy making. Nor did he regard himself temperamentally suited for the task. There were too many paradoxical tensions in his life.

For example, despite his activism, he said, "I long for nothing more than peace and quiet. I have an extraordinary love of harmony, comfort, agreement, and friendly mutual understanding between people; tension, conflict, misunderstanding, uncertainty, and confusion upset me." Despite coming across to many as confident, levelheaded, constant, and equable, "I'm very unsure of myself, almost a neurotic . . . tend to panic easily . . . am plagued by self-doubts." Despite acting (and in some measure being) rational, systematic, and disciplined, "at the same time I'm oversensitive, almost a little sentimental, someone who's always been drawn by everything mysterious . . . inexplicable . . . absurd, everything that escapes order and makes it problematic." Despite appearing a cheerful and sociable person who likes organizing events and bringing people together, "at the same time I'm happiest when alone, and consequently my life is a constant escape into solitude and quiet introspection." Despite being for many a constant source of hope, "I'm always succumbing to depressions, uncertainties, and doubts . . . on the lookout for some encouragement myself." Despite seeming steadfast and brave, if not hardheaded, "the fact is, I'm always afraid of something, and even my alleged courage and stamina spring from fear . . . of my own conscience, which delights in tormenting me for real and imaginary failures."[38]

Though at first he resisted the idea of becoming president, in the end he agreed. It helped, perhaps, that it was not the first time his country had chosen an intellectual for the position. Another factor was the unusual nature of the times. His country was going through a period of transition and needed a publicly identifiable and credible symbolic figure.

Overall, Havel's greatest contribution as a leader is probably his ability to articulate the hunger for meaning among the people in his country and to trace this back to its spiritual source. Doing so has impressed many people in the West, for either they do not hear other national leaders giving voice to this, or, on the rare occasions that they do, the message does not come with the same clarity, passion, and credibility.

Basic Christian Approaches to Spirituality and Leadership

A number of writers on spirituality and work write from a more overtly Christian point of view.[39] In the past, discussions of the role of spirituality in leadership were found in autobiographies of individual leaders. Only in the last decade or two have such discussions appeared in general studies of leadership. Most of these have had leadership in large churches, denominational administration, and Christian organizations in view. One example is Patricia Brown's *Learning to Lead from Your Spiritual Center*.[40] Though her framework is Christian, she focuses mostly on God the Father rather than on Jesus, on humanity's original goodness rather than on the fall, and on the personal gifting of the Spirit rather than on the Spirit's wider presence or activity in the world. In other words, she draws selectively or one-sidedly from central elements of the Christian faith.

Brown argues that the cultivation of one's spirit is central to leadership and is intricately connected to a relationship with God and others. Leadership is fundamentally not something "out there" but something that proceeds from a Spirit-filled center. Honoring this entails taking "the journey in and down" and involves five key affirmations:

1. We are people of worth and live by the Spirit's power, not an official position, and by empowering others, not controlling them.

2. We work through our inner constraints and pains as well as through loving others in a mutual and reconciling way.
3. We are called to live out God's will faithfully and practically as we cocreate and share authority with others.
4. We operate by trust, not manipulation, and out of a vision of wholeness, not a fear of failure.
5. We encounter the transcendent in all parts of creation and experience the fruit of the Spirit in building up character.[41]

These affirmations form the basis for leadership that springs out of who people are rather than what they do or aspire to. They enable people to evaluate whether they are exercising the best kind of leadership; to access their deepest dreams, intuitions, and desires; and to open themselves to new ways God can work in and through them. Grounded in these five affirmations, people engage in what Brown calls "Spiritwork." This involves:

- becoming more integrated and living in the present
- reaching toward intimacy through heart conversations
- connecting body and spirit, family and work
- seeking spiritual guides and mentors
- naming and handling reality in organizations[42]

Max De Pree discusses the attributes of vital organizations and in doing so focuses on the spiritual qualities that give energy through deeply rooted and highly focused leadership.[43] These attributes enrich the life of an organization by encouraging faithfulness to the core values and mission and enhancing its effectiveness in more than purely commercial terms. Such attributes always move an organization toward fulfilling its potential rather than simply attaining its goals. Indeed, they allow people to realize their own potential. Throughout his various writings on leadership, De Pree identifies the following key attributes:

Truth: Truth is personal, and truth is a quality of being, which means it leads to excellence, value, and worth in people and in the work they do. Truth is a difficult concept to pin down, but when we see it or feel it, we know we have encountered it. The great sadness of denying truth is that people become accomplices in their own spiritual demise. In the long-term, this affects the welfare and effectiveness of an organization.

Access: This is a gift that needs to be shared. People should have access to work, a leader, learning opportunities, and medical care. They should also have access to a mentor as well as to faithful and healthy relationships within an organization.

Discipline: It is unfair not to delegate some of the important work. It takes discipline and courage to let go of important work, and it inspires discipline and hard work among followers when they are asked to operate with increased responsibility. A leader has a right to expect discipline from those in an organization and vice versa. In fact, discipline among followers mirrors the discipline demonstrated by leaders.

Accountability: People need accountability, which is different from blame. Blame points the finger of shame; accountability helps people bear the weight of responsibility for outcomes that naturally come with tasks and assignments. Nonprofit organizations are good examples of accountability, for they are intentional about making themselves accountable to the people they serve.

Nourishing of persons: People are nourished by transforming work, growth, learning, and reaching their potential. Only by continuing to renew its members can an organization continually renew itself.

Authenticity: Vital organizations do not grant authenticity; they acknowledge that people (as created in the image of God) are authentic in their being.

Justice: The heart of justice is relationships constructed on right practice. Justice is always related to everyone in an organization; no one can be excluded from this practice. Justice has to do with participation and equal access and is related to the equitable distribution of resources, due process, rights, and responsibility. Justice opens the way for peace—peace and justice go hand in hand.

Respect: This is shown in an organization through civility, good manners, and appropriate language. Respect is evident when everyone is taken seriously. Respect becomes manifest in action.

Hope: Vital organizations generate hope through the way they approach and undertake work in the light of their mission. Organizations that have a clear and compelling mission to which everyone holds themselves accountable create hope in their capacity to realize future dreams. Participation in a worthy mission makes work hopeful and hope-filled. There is a strong correlation between hope and the quality and character of relationships both inside and outside an organization. Organizations that are adept at building relationships that are strong, meaningful, and rich in character are places where hope permeates everything they do.

Unity: Unity transforms organizations into communities. A community performs on a much higher level than an organization because the people in it have a sense of belonging and commitment.

Tolerance: Tolerance is a function of wisdom, discernment, and acceptance. People do not have to think or act alike, but they do have to share a common vision and agreed-on goals for tolerant working relationships to exist.

Simplicity: This is a function of understanding the role of personal restraint in life. Vital organizations draw on resources of the Spirit that enable them to practice conservation and simplicity. These attributes are also essential to renewal and innovation—to take hold of something, a person has to let go of something else.

Beauty and taste: These two qualities nourish the spirits of people and organizations and are keys to creating vitality. Beauty and taste—the opposite of banal—have to do with aesthetics and creativity, poise and quality. People long for that which is beautiful and tasteful. The human spirit is nourished and delighted by beauty and creativity at several levels, in the physical environment, in the quality of the work, in the strength of the relationships in a community, in the poise with which people conduct themselves, and in the level of quality at which an organization operates.

Fidelity to a mission: People show fidelity to a mission through strict observance of their promises, which spring directly from their values. Such fidelity is the realization of commitment: It is words made flesh.

These attributes of vital, life-giving organizations—truth, access, discipline, accountability, the nourishing of persons, authenticity, justice, respect, hope, unity, tolerance, simplicity, beauty and taste, and fidelity to a mission—serve as a call to leaders and followers to create organizations in which people and those they serve can reach their fullest potential. These ideas may appear daunting and at times counter to the conventional wisdom on organizational success because they seem to focus on the "soft side" rather than on typical activities such as developing a strategy, improving work tasks, and building competitive advantage. In point of fact, these attributes pave the way for personal and organization success, particularly in today's competitive marketplace. Perhaps these attributes can best serve as "fruits of the Spirit" for organizational life.

Conclusion

Though, as mentioned, Brown's approach is an overtly Christian one, its understanding of spirituality is limited and inadequate and fails to draw on the full range of biblical and theological resources that are available. Interestingly, Vaill, who has a less overtly religious view of spirit, is the one who highlights the importance of the theological as well as the spiritual dimension of leadership. De Pree gives flesh to a Christian approach to spirituality and leadership in talking about the attributes of vital organizations in a way that echoes but also translates for the contemporary workplace a number of core theological convictions.

The following chapter of this book seeks to give more substance to the spiritual dimension of leadership as it considers writings that draw more fully or explicitly on specific religious perspectives.

popular and more substantial faith-based approaches to leadership

Most writers on leadership do not look to religious sources or tradition for inspiration. Instead, they rely on established theories of leadership, on personal or observed experience, or on empirical studies of how leadership works. While they often include ethical maxims that stem from a particular religious tradition, for the most part they are not aware that separating a saying from its framework weakens its effectiveness. Recently, however, writers on leadership have begun to draw on religious traditions more broadly. A number have turned to Eastern and/or New Age spirituality.[1] Others, several of whom are discussed below, draw on Jewish and Christian sources.[2]

Some Popular Faith-based Approaches to Leadership

David Baron: A Liberal-Jewish Approach

David Baron is a successful businessman and the founder of a liberal, as opposed to a more traditional Orthodox, Jewish synagogue in Beverly Hills that serves people principally in the worlds of media and finance. His book *Moses on Management: Leadership Lessons from the Greatest Manager of All Time* focuses on the pivotal Jewish religious leader Moses, drawing lessons from his life and work for the way leaders should operate today.[3] In doing this, he identifies various parallels between the uncertainties and challenges of Moses' world and ours. His treatment contains a blend of Bible exposition, contemporary anecdotes, and humorous insights into the dynamics of leadership.

In the preface, Baron asserts that, contrary to popular belief, the Bible is all about business, and he declares that Moses was the greatest manager of all time. Though Moses suffered from what today would be regarded as significant drawbacks—he was reluctant, inarticulate, contradictory, sometimes impulsive, and occasionally overreached himself—he exhibited impressive strengths and achievements. He was not born to a leadership role, nor was he especially charismatic. He did not lead from the top, and he avoided control or manipulation. Though not the complete spiritual or moral role model, Moses was an inspired, hands-on, and effective leader who managed a consistently uncooperative staff and handled hostile outside competition. He grew into his role through a time of patient preparation and experience on the job, and his faith in God and humility before others were the cornerstones of his approach. He possessed such crucial skills as flexibility, quick thinking, confidence building, and the ability to forge unity out of a diverse group. He was also able to train and pass these skills on to others.

Next, Baron deals with issues of motivation and communication, Moses' tactics for mobilizing and energizing his people through their long journey, and the key ethical guidelines he laid out. He suggests parallels between the roundabout way Moses led Israel to the Promised Land and nonlinear approaches to business strategy, and between the role of the Ten Commandments in Israel's life and mission statements in organizations today. He summarizes Moses' success as a leader with the following ten phrases:

> Accept the role of leadership. Assess the situation. Connect with God and the people around you. Deliver the results. Persevere through difficulties. Solve problems as they arise. Search out stimulating people and ideas. Enforce the organization's rules. Endow your people with a legacy. Know when it is time to leave.[4]

Baron recognizes some of the limits and weaknesses of leaders. He includes sections on learning to take reproof as well as mete it out, seeking help from within the leader's family, not being blinded by one's own power, letting others share the burden, being responsible for the hazards one creates, and making oneself as accessible as possible to those who take a different view. The ethical code he establishes goes beyond moral rules and includes such important items as being an advocate for one's people, speaking out against oppressors and wrongdoers, defending justice but not for the reward, blending compassion with accountability, creating a hospitable environment, and remembering the importance of small gestures.

One weakness in the book from a Christian point of view is his talk of Moses' "inventing" or "creating" a moral compass and strategic procedures for his people.

Such language devalues the role of God in these two areas, though Baron does recognize the presence of divine revelation in the giving of the Ten Commandments. He regularly refers to God in discussing both Moses' and present leadership, but his discussion of the regulations of the covenant and holiness codes in the Books of Exodus and Leviticus suggests that these came from Moses' own mind. As a result, Baron's approach contains a humanistic element that is at odds with the biblical material.

Laura Beth Jones and Charles Manz: A Para-Denominational Christian Approach

Laura Beth Jones is the founder and president of the Jones Group, an advertising, marketing, and business development firm whose mission is "to recognize, promote, and inspire divine excellence." She identifies her religious tradition as a mixture of Presbyterianism, Methodism, and ecumenical Christianity. Her book *Jesus CEO: Using Ancient Wisdom for Visionary Leadership,* which was twenty years in the making, is intended to be "a practical, step-by-step guide to communicating with and motivating people."[5] Her main interest is the types of skills involved in self-mastery, action, and relationships that Jesus utilized to train and catalyze his team. Throughout she weaves together the ethical principles and the general guidelines that were integral to Jesus' approach.

Jones labels Jesus' approach the Omega Management Style, distinguishing it from the Alpha and Beta Management Styles associated with authoritative masculine and cooperative feminine uses of power. The Omega style is characterized by: (1) the unparalleled success of Jesus' training of just twelve people, given the extent of his influence today, (2) the very human, unqualified, diverse, and fractious group he had with him, and (3) the applicability of Jesus' leadership style to any group of people involved in a common task. She believes that Jesus' Omega approach transcends the other two management styles, primarily because of the way it harnesses and empowers each person's spiritual energy.

Jones's concluding affirmations for leaders draw together the key elements of her book.[6] Aspects of them are highly revealing. For example, almost seventy affirmations begin with the word *I* (never *we*), and only seven contain a reference to God. This individualistic tone is strange given the book's focus on Jesus. Many of the principles she derives from Jesus' life and work are valid ones—being clear about one's mission, not requiring or seeking others' approval, looking at situations in new and different ways, having passion for a cause, holding others accountable for their actions, empowering others through one's example, and seeing the praise of others as the number one priority. She also specifically mentions the importance of seeing others as gifts of God and of recognizing that only God knows the total plan.

Yet some of her statements are couched in self-serving language. "I accomplish difficult tasks for my training and strengthening." "I release others so that I myself can fly." "I judge no one, knowing that judging others causes major energy leaks in my life." "I serve others, knowing that . . . I too will be well served." Also, Jones, drawing lessons from Jesus' so-called self-mastery to serve as a guide for one's own self-mastery, introduces a humanistic note that is not present in the Gospels. Jesus was wholly oriented to God, not self, as his clear statements about "doing the Father's will" (John 6:38) demonstrate.[7]

In addition, Jones's reference to transparency mentions only one's strengths, not one's weaknesses. Indeed, there is almost a complete denial of inadequacies and struggles, and it is only success, never failure, that receives mention. This is odd given the fate Jesus suffered on the cross, despite the ultimate outcome of his death. It is also one-sided for leaders to be told that "Jesus had no ambivalence about what he wanted to do,"[8] given Jesus' request in the Garden of Gethsemane that the cup be taken from him (Matt. 26:39). Nor is it helpful for leaders to be told "to believe in themselves 100%."[9] Only an American could have written the fourth affirmation: "I shape my own destiny. What I believe, I become. What I become, I can do."[10]

Another book that promotes an ecumenical Christian approach to leadership is *The Leadership Wisdom of Jesus: Practical Lessons for Today* by Charles Manz.[11] As the preface makes clear, Manz proposes a multi-faith approach that, while it focuses on Jesus, seeks to transcend race and religion. Though many of Jesus' teachings do not directly address leadership, Manz is convinced that they offer a depth of ethical and practical guidance for leadership practice. He suggests that leaders should take account of the form as well as the content of many of Jesus' teachings, such as his use of parables. Because Jesus' framework is ultimately one of life beyond death, Manz recognizes that his injunctions are not necessarily intended to pay off in this life. Yet he believes that at some level all people desire to have a positive spiritual connection with others. Within this framework, he looks at leading others with compassion, leading others to be their best selves, how the seeds of greatness lie in the power of small things, and the importance of empowering others rather than being a visionary.

It is not improper to look to Jesus' person and work for guidance in exercising leadership, but one must see the full framework and nature of Jesus' approach to do this properly. Manz recognizes the indirect nature of some of Jesus' teaching about leadership as well as his otherworldly orientation. While not focusing too much on the person of the leader, Manz does see a positive spiritual orientation in both leaders and followers. He therefore fails to acknowledge the dark side of human nature. He also overlooks the differences in cultural conditions and even styles of speaking between first-century Jews and twenty-first-century Americans. This leads him to interpret some of Jesus' teaching in contemporary Westernized terms.

Max De Pree, formerly CEO and chairman of the board of Herman Miller Furniture Co., draws discreetly but firmly on his Reformed Protestant religious heritage. Other influences on his view of leadership include his army experience during World War II, his work experience at Herman Miller, and people such as the businessman Robert Greenleaf and the artist Charles Eames.

Ultimately, De Pree's spiritual journey deeply shaped his core perspectives, values, and commitments. This is revealed in the language he uses, the policies he framed, and the procedures he designed. His approach emphasizes (1) serving, which involves making oneself vulnerable to others' points of view and criticisms; (2) abandoning one's ego and depending on the expertise of others; (3) creating environments in which people can grow and develop; (4) and communicating that invites input and involvement.

In his key writings on leadership, De Pree identifies a range of attributes of good leadership.[12] Some of these have to do with gaining wisdom (e.g., intellectual curiosity and energy, discernment that brings insight and judgment). Others focus on developing relationships (e.g., having an awareness of people's cares, yearnings, and struggles; being present to them; having trust in their abilities; and having a willingness to be vulnerable). Others concern character (e.g., integrity, courage, dependability, and honesty). Several have to do with one's worldview (e.g., being comfortable with ambiguity; moving to and fro between future, past, and present; and having a sense of humor). Though largely implicit in his writings, it is clear that De Pree believes these attributes operate within a fundamental framework of belief.

A basic feature of his all-embracing theological framework is the conviction, derived from the Book of Genesis, that everyone is created "in God's image" (Gen. 1:26). This means that each person reflects the Maker in a unique way and must be treated with respect and dignity. Leaders have the responsibility of helping people become who they can be and of opening themselves to learn from them. Since God creates diversity among people, leaders should endeavor to recognize and empower it so that everyone can make a unique contribution. Part of this entails viewing each person as a whole person, not simply a worker, and valuing people over programs, systems, and bureaucracy. Because creativity and innovation lie at the heart of God's act of making people in his image, these attributes exist in every person, and leaders ought to enhance them.

De Pree also has a strong sense of God's operating by way of covenantal relationships. This was at the heart of God's bond with Israel. It involved more than a contractual arrangement through which each party sets parameters and conditions regarding what they will do for the other. Such an arrangement, if broken, leads to a termination of the link between the parties. Instead, God made an unconditional commitment to Israel and later to those who became Jesus' followers. Though both the Jews and Jesus' disciples had obligations, they stemmed from love, not law, and when broken did not necessarily end the relationship. De Pree saw his relationship with his employees as potentially a lifelong one and his responsibility as nurturing, enhancing, and supporting them through all kinds of circumstances. This created a space for his workers where they had a sense of belonging; could be and become themselves; were invited to participate in envisioning, designing, and implementing the company's future; and were held compassionately but professionally accountable.[13]

For De Pree, justice and equity are also strong values. These motifs appear often in the Bible, especially in the prophetic writings, wisdom literature, and Gospels. Embodying these in the workplace entails: (1) discerning the realities inside and outside the workplace and basing all that happens on truth telling, (2) striving to make decisions and policies that promote the common good of everyone in it, (3) being concerned about the poor and disadvantaged members of the organization, and (4) compensating and rewarding people in an equitable way. Employees should also be encouraged to help eliminate the needs and challenges of the wider society. Because the environment should also be dealt with in a responsible way, organizations should give careful consideration to the way facilities are built and settings developed, providing attractive and functional surroundings for employees.[14]

Finally, De Pree's view of leadership revolves around the core values of the Christian faith. First, trust in others is paramount, for without it an organization cannot function effectively. For employees, this involves developing a sense of loyalty when the actions of the company justify it. For employers, it means ensuring that the central values of the company are represented in its treatment of workers. Second, leaders should care about the welfare of their employees as workers but more fundamentally as people who have other roles and responsibilities. This includes giving them consideration and support when unexpected challenges, including long-term illness or corporate downsizing, arise. Third, leaders should both articulate and embody hope, cultivating and exemplifying this through inspiring vision and creating synergy among their followers.

At the heart of these core values is integrity, which should govern all that takes place. This embraces fidelity to the mission of the organization, keeping one's word and fulfilling one's promises, and making only justified and defensible, not opportunistic or self-serving, compromises that are in the best interests of people. What flows from putting first things first is excellence at all levels of the operation and effectiveness in the organization's core business and outcomes.[15]

More Substantial Theological Treatments of Leadership

A CHRIST-CENTERED APPROACH TO LEADERSHIP

Many books on leadership in the church focus on Jesus as the exemplary role model. For example, Andrew Le Peau's *Paths of Leadership,* referencing James MacGregor Burns's work on transforming leadership, focuses on Jesus as an exemplar of serving, following, facilitating, teaching, modeling, and envisioning.[16] A few books written by Christians include reference to activities outside the church but generally make little mention of people's work and workplaces. Leighton Ford's *Jesus: The Transforming Leader* does mention these settings more than most, even if only in a secondary way.[17]

Ford's book offers a conversation between the portrait of Jesus in the Gospels and the model of transformational leadership articulated by Warren Bennis and Burt Nanus (discussed earlier). Ford bookends his portrait of Jesus by pointing out what was distinctive about him, namely, he was the unique Son of God, the Savior, and sovereign. In the intervening chapters, he points to nine roles involved in Jesus' leadership that are indispensable to transforming leadership. These are:

1. *the strategist:* In this role, Jesus had a sense of destiny; fulfilled earlier promises and hopes; had a consistent kingdom strategy and a long-range global goal; and leveraged the contribution of a few for a wider group of people.
2. *the seeker:* As the seeker, Jesus promoted kingdom values; served another's cause; taught another's truth; accepted another's results; awaited another's time; and dreamed of another's glory.
3. *the seer:* As the seer, Jesus experienced vision at key points. This vision had a divine source and was practical, compelling, personal, radical, realistic, and yet hopeful.
4. *the strong one:* In this role, Jesus showed his strength of character; external power and inner authority; firmness of purpose; force of speech; and gentleness, sensitivity, patience, and decisiveness. He was also accessible yet needed to withdraw at times.
5. *the servant:* Jesus was on assignment from God; inverted the world's power scale; and showed the strength of servant power, the force of example, his mission to suffer, and the power of the cross.
6. *the shepherd-maker:* In this role, Jesus was the recruiter and empowerer; shared life as the prime curriculum; formed a team with a common life and goal; enabled others to find meaning, equality, enthusiasm, and growth; and shared risks, a future, and power.

7. *the spokesperson:* As the spokesperson, Jesus was the prime communicator; modeled communication through clarity of purpose and confidence; was sensitive to words; respected means and ends; and evidenced focused speech, wise timing, and a sense of boundaries.
8. *the struggler:* In this role, Jesus discerned and transformed conflict; revealed strategies for fundamental, unavoidable, essential, and incidental conflict; handled rejection; and showed discretion and discernment.
9. *the sustainer:* As the sustainer, Jesus employed the key strategies of showing the way, shaping people, symbolizing values, setting the stage, and ultimately sharing the Spirit with others.

A look at this list reveals marks of Jesus' leadership that would not transfer to most organizations today, whether based on Christian principles or not.

- Pursuing a kingdom orientation and strategy. While there may be elements of such a strategy and orientation in some contemporary organizations, what is more important is looking at ways work and workplaces can reflect God's everyday work through building community, seeking justice, and serving needs.
- Having a mission to suffer. While suffering may be a potential by-product of a faith-based approach to leadership, it is not part of its overt purpose and will not necessarily have a kind of "redemptive" effect.
- Awaiting another's time and dreaming of another's glory. While a sense of timing and a degree of modesty are key to effective leadership, to some extent, leaders' schedules do not always leave them much room to maneuver. There are also stakeholders, and often stockholders, to take into account.
- Experiencing divine vision at key points. For ordinary leaders, vision is not purely an individual matter and does not come as clearly from a divine source. It tends to come in ways that involve the collaboration of others in its pursuit, evaluation, and framing.
- Handling fundamental and unavoidable conflict. Leaders are not as central or as crucial to the life of organizations as Jesus was to the Christian movement. There is always the option of resignation if their—or the organization's—integrity is in danger of being compromised.
- Strength of character and force of speech. While both are admirable aspirations, leaders do not have access to the Spirit "without measure" (John 3:34) in the way Jesus did. Even in the Bible, some leaders were either in need of a colleague more gifted at communicating (Moses) or failed to possess conventional eloquence (Paul).
- Inverting the world's power scale. While believers seek to live in ways that are in tension with the way power is often employed in the world,

leaders—even Christian leaders—have to operate in ways that correlate to some extent with the surrounding practices.

- Shared life as the prime curriculum. While a case may be made for theological students to be trained as they live together in a residential setting,[18] it is unrealistic for most work teams to have a common life as well as common work.
- Sensitivity to and shaping of others. The resources for developing insight into and properly handling others are not available to leaders today as they were to Jesus. This is also true of sharing the Spirit with people in comparison with modeling a life indwelt by the Spirit or helping people catch the spirit of an organization.

These differences between Jesus' leadership and that of leaders today do not mean that the work and setting of certain individuals do not in some ways parallel what Jesus did and experienced. Nor do they mean that leaders cannot learn from Jesus' life and approach. Because of Jesus' unique status and calling, however, the correlation between today's work and his is less than some writers suggest.

These same kinds of limitations are present in the books by Laura Beth Jones, Charles Manz, and Bob Bruner mentioned earlier. They approach Jesus even more uncritically through the lens of modern Western assumptions, especially by individualizing the content and application of Jesus' approach. Even Leighton Ford is vulnerable, as his omission of Jesus' healing and miraculous powers indicates. Jones and Manz apply his teachings and practices without sufficient reference to actual work structures and processes.

One way of scrutinizing the extent to which contemporary assumptions creep into such approaches is to check them against distinctly unmodern characteristics of Jesus' way of operating. Take, for example, the classic book *The Peril of Modernizing Jesus*, by the Quaker New Testament scholar Henry Cadbury. According to Cadbury, our age is perhaps more different from Jesus' time in its ways of thinking than in its ways of operating. "Manufacture, transportation, communication we know to be now quite different: but do we realize how different [are] mental processes, intellectual assumptions, forms of self-consciousness?"[19] He adds, "Not even the use of Jesus' own terms prevents an almost complete modernizing of him. In fact to use them in a modern sense only deceives ourselves and others into thinking that we are accurately representing him."[20] An extreme example of this is Bruce Barton's *The Man Nobody Knows*, according to which Jesus exemplified all the principles of modern salesmanship. "He was, of course, a good mixer; he made contacts easily and was quick to get *en rapport* with his 'prospect.' He appreciated the advertising value of news and so called his message 'good news.' His habit of rising early was indicative of the high pressure of the 'go-getter' so necessary for a successful career."[21]

Cadbury goes on to suggest some less recognized ways in which Jesus' general outlook and method of operating differed from those today. He has in mind the managerial mind-set and organizational culture that pervade modern society, the preoccupation with outcomes and success, and the preoccupation with structural change and reform.

First, Jesus' life was not as strategized or as organized as people tend to think. Modern culture's emphasis on making a living, carefully apportioning time, and planning for the future was largely absent from Jesus' world. "We can hardly make a picture of Jesus' life and that of his contemporaries that will be too casual for the facts. . . . Jesus was much more a vagabond or gipsy than many another in the land."[22] Indeed, "he reacted to situations as they arose but probably he hardly had a program or a plan. . . . The religious man in particular leaves planning to God and simply submits to the inevitable. He may foresee it, but that is not the same thing as courting it or planning it."[23] While Jesus' relationship with and submission to God certainly gave his life both a trajectory and a unity, his life did not involve the degree of creative planning and calculated prioritizing people tend to assume.

Second, we cannot read Jesus' teaching without considering "how far the traits of character or circumstances described tend to produce particular outcomes, for example, blessing or success." We "regard him as an experienced observer of the laws of character, which he states with insight and understanding of their inevitable results. I do not wish to claim that there are no such laws or that they are not in accord with Jesus' standards, but . . . for Jesus . . . the blessing is personally bestowed," that is, by divine intervention.[24]

Third, Jesus rarely if ever dealt with such institutions as work, private property, and wealth or with social groups along status or class lines. As far as social interrelations are concerned, "the modern mind tries to deal with both parties at once and to rise into a plane or principle of action which takes the interests, privileges, rights, or duties of both into view. Jesus appears to think conversely of one man at a time. . . . Even the Golden Rule . . . is merely advice for each man by himself."[25] Jesus did not universalize this so that it became a principle of organizational interaction.

Fourth and most striking of all, the conspicuous absences in Jesus' teaching is the appeal to social motive. "Sometimes he appeals to no motive at all, demanding a self-sacrifice that asks no return. . . . At other times he appeals to men's own sense of what is right. . . . In a few passages he is represented as urging a religious motive . . . or dedication to [his] person or cause. . . . Frequently the only motive is what we would now call a self-regarding motive, but nowhere—and this is my point—do I find unmistakable appeal to the rights or needs of the other party."[26]

Other Christian ethicists today have been influenced by John Yoder and have come to more radical conclusions about the nature of Jesus' values and goals. The best known of these is probably Stanley Hauerwas.[27] These authors rightly point out the provocatively prophetic character of many of Jesus' actions and teachings, which only heightens the difficulty of casting him in executive leadership terms. They also highlight the important and seminal role of the Christian community as an exemplar for contemporary Christians.[28] Yet while their approach is rightly critical of some of the uses to which Jesus is put in discussions of leadership, the differences between Jesus' mission and that of Christians today must not be overly emphasized.

TRINITARIAN APPROACHES TO LEADERSHIP

Christian Schumacher, son of the widely read E. F. Schumacher, has advanced the idea of viewing the Godhead as a model for integrating faith and work. For him, the Trinity of Father, Son, and Spirit models the activities of planning, implementing, and evaluating that are part of any good workplace structure.[29] In some respects, his approach echoes Dorothy Sayers's *Mind of the Maker*.[30] In this stimulating book, Sayers develops an analogy between the Trinity and the act of creation involving the interrelationship of idea, activity, and energy.

At a more sophisticated theological level, the Australian Christian ethicist Gordon Preece takes issue with those who view human work as connected primarily with the work of the Father, or of the Son, or of the Spirit.[31] He argues that human work is in some sense an expression of all three—the creative and providential activity of the Father, the servant and redemptive work of the Son, and the charismatic and transformative work of the Spirit. Preece is indebted in part to the thoughtful, if somewhat abstract, theological discussion of human work in *Work in the Spirit: Toward a Theology of Work* by Miroslav Volf. Volf, in turn, was influenced by his mentor, the influential Protestant theologian Jurgen Moltmann, who drew attention to the relevance of the Trinity for understanding government. Put simply, the Trinity does not support what he calls a hierarchical or chain of command approach but rather a perichoretic and collegial approach.[32]

Catherine Mowry LaCugna's *God for Us: The Trinity and Christian Life* discusses the Trinity in a way that illuminates an understanding of the nature of persons and the ethics of relationships in organizations.[33] For LaCugna, inclusiveness, community, and freedom are the ethical values that find their origin in the interrelationality within the Trinity. These three ways of relating should characterize human relationships in organizations and are especially important for affirming those who work within them.

Inclusiveness speaks to accepting and welcoming people into a group or organization. Leaders who practice inclusion accept people in their uniqueness and create a sense of belonging by showing interest in discovering their particular character and gifts. By providing a hospitable space for people to actively participate, a leader unleashes a flow of resources and possibilities into an organization.

A community seeks to acknowledge interrelatedness at every level of reality and contradicts the forces destructive to genuine community, especially the misuse of power and discrimination. In recent years, much has been written about Peter Senge's idea of the learning organization.[34] According to Russ Moxley, from the Center for Creative Leadership, the learning organization and building community go hand in hand.[35] The same principles that generate the learning organization—interdependence in decision making and problem solving, dialogue and acceptance of differences—also create a sense of community for its members. Leaders play a key role in creating organizations in which everyone can contribute, learn, and develop both personally and professionally. This offers people a context for participating not just in a company but in a community.

Freedom refers to personhood in a community. It allows people to contribute uniquely and authentically, to express creativity, and to operate within a safe environment of trust and hope. Max De Pree has said that "leaders owe people space, space in the sense of freedom. Freedom in the sense of enabling our gifts to be exercised, the need to give each other the space to grow, to be ourselves, to exercise our diversity."[36]

According to Peter Block and Peter Koestenbaum in *Freedom and Accountability at Work: Applying Philosophical Insight to the Real World,* to embrace freedom is to accept accountability, and with accountability comes guilt, and with guilt comes anxiety. And so we seek to "escape from freedom," as Erich Fromm put it,[37] so that we might escape the anxiety that comes with freedom. We escape through conformity, disrespect for individual differences, and dominating regimes.

To create the space for freedom will at times require initiating and leading change. To many people, such change feels more like an act of intrusion or disruption than of personal or organizational liberation. In fact, however, it is an act of love because it brings people in the organization and the way the organization operates closer to the essence of the inner life of God in the Trinity. Leadership that creates freedom requires a movement beyond the overly rigid boundaries most organizations seem to have. Such a movement—motivated by love—opens up for the leader and the followers the experience and the practice of freedom in the workplace. The inclusive and communal character of the interrelationships within the Trinity, when lived out in an organization, serve the people in spiritual as well as practical ways.

Stacy Rinehart's *Upside Down: The Paradox of Servant Leadership*[38] focuses primarily on leadership in parachurch movements or Christian organizations and stresses that relationship is at the core of the Godhead. The basic spiritual principles of leadership are enshrined within this divine relationship. The members of the Trinity work together in developing the plan of redemption, exhibiting interdependence, unity, and diversity. There is role differentiation, but the members share authority. Lessons leaders can learn from this include:

- There should be unity and diversity among leaders. Leadership should be multiple, not single, with shared authority.
- Leadership should be relational, not hierarchical or organizational. Relationships, not the task of an organization, should bind leaders to followers. Power struggles, jealousy, and competition have no place. Each person has a unique and complementary role and contribution.
- Mutual respect and dependence are spiritual requisites of leadership. As people listen more carefully to one another and discern more clearly the value of one another's contributions, leadership begins to take place through more than one person. Leadership rotates according to whoever is pointing the best way forward at a particular time.[39]

Rinehart argues that such a model of leadership also has servanthood rather than mastery over others at its center.

A more developed trinitarian perspective on leadership is present in a book on leadership in both the church and the world by Benjamin Williams and Michael McKibben.[40] These coauthors write out of their managerial and consulting experience and have the everyday world as well as official religious work in mind. What makes their contribution interesting is the way it draws on Orthodox rather than Protestant or Catholic traditions.

Williams and McKibben's basic concern is that believers "have fallen prey to a myriad of leadership theories, experiments, and philosophies which are, at best, only partially Christian." Similar to Robert Greenleaf, they view leadership as in some measure "the responsibility of all and the charge of some." They describe leadership in action as "perceiving and articulating the vision of the kingdom of God and effectively defining and communicating its incarnation, following Christ's example of service." They see a reflection of this in Christ's community, the church, the body of Christ.[41]

Having a clear sense of who one is, which comes through developing intimacy with God, is where leadership begins. Knowing oneself is the key to one's effectiveness as a leader. Because we are created in the image of God, we reflect something of the life of the Trinity. Because leadership takes place within the Trinity, it is in essence "a divine attribute" that is at the very heart of our being. It is a God-given dynamic in our nature and therefore a basic dimension of being a person. This is a democratic understanding of leadership. As the authors say, "Our leadership positions may vary and our positions of leadership may be different, but that doesn't alter the fact that we are all called to be leaders." The goal of leadership is "enabling persons to become all that they were created to be."[42]

Vision is at the root of discerning and implementing this understanding. A proper vision entails having a clear mental picture of how things should be, regardless of what they are now. It involves loving God and the creation and desiring to live a life of thanksgiving for all that God is and has done. As a result, people with this vision accept the responsibility of stewardship, which involves the human management of God's gift of the world. Such a vision gives aim to daily life, guides commitment, stimulates motivation, informs speech and behavior, clarifies expectations, and develops unity.

The Father is the source of the vision, Jesus models its implementation, and the Spirit generates enthusiasm and empowerment for it. The unity, love, and harmony among the three members of the Trinity exemplify and catalyze the process and structures involved in a vision coming into being. As people work together to discern and implement a vision—working through the mission, goals, objectives, projects, activities, and procedures involved—they are engaged in a trinitarian exercise that issues in incarnated action in the church and the world. The Persons of the Trinity act together, in unique but inseparable ways, and never do anything apart from one another. Leaders must seek a similar kind of participation in organizations. The goal is consensus, not merely agreement but a common position reached as people possessing varying levels of authority engage in conversation.

It is clear that for these authors the Trinity is not a doctrinal abstraction but a divine paradigm of what leadership involves. Trinitarian dynamics, therefore, have practical implications for how leadership functions. First, it should never be authoritarian, coercive, or dictatorial. Love and service, not command and control, characterize relations within the life of the Godhead. A trinitarian view of leadership also navigates between hierarchical (top-down) and egalitarian (leaderless team) styles of leadership. In the Trinity, the Father is the source of its life, but all three members of the Trinity act in a unified, loving, and harmonious or conciliar way. Leaders must strive to fuse these apparent opposites. According to Williams and McKibben, the former has more to do with the structure of decision making, the latter with its communication, both of which are needed for effective leadership and mutual accountability.

The authors identify other theological motifs as a framework for understanding and practicing leadership. First, leaders should view all of life as sacramental so that every activity can become a participation in and a reflection of divine life at work. Leadership can be viewed as a sacramental activity because "it includes the opportunity and responsibility to serve and to be *the channel* for communion, love, and grace."[43] Second, leaders should view Christ as the servant leader par excellence, reflected especially in his washing of the disciples' feet, his role as the suffering servant, and his self-emptying sacrifice on the cross. It is important to note, however, that the model of servant leadership Jesus provides is based on his following the Father. Leading and following, therefore, are two sides of the same coin. A leader is a first among equals rather than a person on the dominant side of an unequal relationship. Such leadership involves authority, but authority that flows from love, and function revolving around service rather than positions and power.

Rinehart's approach rightly puts relationship at the heart of the Trinity and draws appropriate implications for leadership. Leaders should demonstrate interdependence, exhibit unity in diversity, recognize people's unique contributions, and express shared authority. Yet by ruling out a hierarchical element by stressing the equality of those in leadership, he makes the Trinity too egalitarian. He also bypasses an identifiable human authority in favor of emphasizing the ultimate leadership of the Godhead, thereby overlooking the need for leadership to be represented symbolically if not actually in human representatives.

Williams and McKibben's approach goes further, taking some of these inadequacies into account and providing a more nuanced trinitarian perspective. Still, their treatment has a few problems.

- Their terminology is not always user-friendly. Part of the reason for this is that the book comes from within an Orthodox setting and the authors have a desire to address people with Orthodox convictions. In addition, the Orthodox worldview, even when it is engaging with aspects of daily life, often seems a little disengaged from many of the realities of contemporary challenges in the workplace.
- Their failure to interact with the contemporary discourse on leadership in the workplace limits the value of their work.
- They include little recognition or discussion of some of the harsher pressures and realities of working life. This too limits the value of their discussion.

Despite the inadequacies in the trinitarian approaches to leadership, they do provide an illuminating alternative to understanding roles, work, and leadership. By exploring the multifaceted relationships within the Trinity, it is possible to glean insight and new models for shared power, relating to others, and leading. The nature of God, expressed in the Trinity, offers a superb representation of unity within diversity, community, freedom, and a collegial approach that is nonhierarchical. Since we are created in the image of God, we are drawn to a way of leading that honors the nature of God as expressed in the Trinity. People begin to experience the sacramental nature of leading when leadership takes on the nature of God.

A LIFE-STORY APPROACH TO LEADERSHIP

In addition to concentrating on Jesus or the Trinity, other writers draw attention to a wide range of biblical figures who can illumine an understanding of leadership from a theological point of view. Numerous biblical stories feature leaders of God's people, focusing on significant moments in their lives and work or providing extensive accounts of their development as leaders. Interesting examples of leaders with civic as well as religious responsibilities are David, Solomon, and

Hezekiah. John Goldingay, in his down-to-earth portrayal of David's reign in *Men Behaving Badly*,[44] describes in graphic and unapologetic terms the weaknesses and strengths, blind spots and awareness, compromises and integrity, failures and achievements of David as a man, head of a family, and ruler. In his book titled *Relational Leadership: A Biblical Model for Influence and Service*, Walter Wright focuses on the character and activities of some lesser-known biblical figures, such as Philemon, Tychicus, and Onesimus.[45]

J. Robert Clinton has given perhaps the most detailed attention to biblical figures in regard to leadership. In his work on developing a philosophy of leadership, he identifies a number of typical stages and tests through which effective leaders pass on their way to fulfilling their roles.[46] Not all leaders pass through all stages or in the same order. Indeed, Clinton's typology runs the risk of being overly systematized. Yet it offers some interesting insights into the process of leadership development.

While the Bible is at the heart of Clinton's approach, it is not the only resource he uses. Scripture, he says, is the leadership anchor, but it "does not speak directly to all issues of leadership," and "when it does speak there is freedom. It often gives general ideas or specific examples from which a leader must be led by the Holy Spirit to applications."[47] Clinton draws on a wide range of biblical examples, including Moses, Joshua, David, Jeremiah, and Barnabas. He also studies a large number of historical figures, mostly people in professional Christian ministries with a pastoral or missionary orientation, as well as some contemporary figures. He writes primarily for those in pastoral and missionary work, and his overall goal is to help potential and existing leaders organize what is happening in their lives, anticipate what may develop, understand new possibilities in past events, and better order their lives.

Clinton identifies the three components of his "leadership emergence framework." These are time analysis, process items, and patterns of response.

Time analysis concerns the general trajectory of a leader's development and provides the broader framework within which significant experiences in leadership formation take place. Time analysis refers to the chronological development of a leader and enables an emerging leader to see stages of development in relation to the whole, integrate experiences into a coherent picture, and help set expectations for the future. Though each leader's time line is unique, the emerging patterns and overall lessons can be compared to a generalized ministry time line, which facilitates a wider orientation and evaluation of a leader's development. Such a time line moves through three stages.

1. A ministry foundation is established between the mid-teenage years and late young adulthood.
2. Next follows a growth in ministry, lasting anywhere from ten to twenty-five years, in which the primary thrust is the growth of the leader rather than ministry outcomes.

3. Finally, a person experiences a unique ministry, a time of effective work that generally comes in early to late midlife. This is usually preceded by a period of difficulty that opens up the opportunity for a deepened relationship with God and greater character development.

Process items describe incidents in a leader's life through which God shapes him or her. Though each person is unique and each situation is specific, some common elements appear in the journey toward leadership.

Some incidents form character and involve the crucial role of "integrity checks." A successful story is the challenge to their food laws faced by Daniel and his friends (Daniel 1). A failure is Saul's refusal to fulfill God's directions in battle (1 Samuel 15). Variants on this are "obedience checks," such as are found in the story of Abraham's offering of Isaac (Genesis 22), and "word checks," which assess how much a potential leader has understood God. The classic example of this is Samuel's message from God (1 Samuel 3).

In the early phase of work for God, people are generally confronted with two "ministry processes." The first is a ministry challenge, such as that confronted by Paul and Barnabas in Antioch before they received their main missionary call (Acts 11). A ministry challenge is a simple assignment that focuses on the job to be carried out as well as its effect on the leader and those associated with him or her. In the middle phase of maturing, a second ministry process involving ministry training often takes place, a good example of which is Timothy's recruitment by and accompanying of Paul (Acts 16). Discovery of a person's key giftedness often takes place during this time, as was Barnabas's experience in understanding the special contribution of Paul (Acts 9:27), which became pivotal for Barnabas's own future missionary role alongside the apostle.

Other process items have to do with what Clinton calls "relationship learning." These incidents in a leader's life teach valuable lessons about working with others and provide positive and negative insights into how spiritual authority functions. James and John encountered this type of incident when they requested status alongside Jesus (Matt. 20:20–28). Encounters with the changing dynamics of leadership, as with the shift of focus from Barnabas to Paul (beginning with Acts 13:13), as well as lessons about relating effectively to colleagues, also fit this category. Also relevant here is how to deal with ministry conflicts between subgroups, such as Greek and Hebrew Christians (Acts 6:1), and leadership backlashes, as Paul himself experienced (2 Corinthians 10).

Another set of process items requires discernment in dealing with specific challenges relating to faith, influence, and prayer. According to Clinton, while these process items can be analyzed separately, they need to be correlated with such wider issues as development of leadership capacity and responsibility, expansion of effectiveness, and followership, all of which are basic to a biblical perspective on leadership.

In the final phase of ministry, leaders often face a set of experiences that are difficult to negotiate but open doors to more profound experiences of God. These include enforced isolation due to sickness, imprisonment, organizational pressures, or even self-evaluation. An example of the second is Paul's imprisonment in Ephesus. Leaders may also face significant crises, at times of a life-threatening nature, that help to form a mature character. Instructive here are the events Paul refers to in 2 Corinthians 1:8–11 and 4:7–12.

Because guidance has to do with the whole of a leader's life, the process items connected with it fall into different parts of the time line. Among these are the divine contacts God arranges, such as Paul's meeting Aquila and Priscilla (Acts 18), or mentors that have a profound influence on a person's life, as Barnabas did with Paul (Acts 11). Divine affirmation occurs when there is a special indication from God of his authoritative presence with a person, as with the miraculous answer to Samuel's prayer (1 Sam. 12:13–19). There is also what Clinton calls "dual confirmation," or two ways of receiving confirmation about a particular direction, such as Paul experienced first on the road to Damascus (Acts 9:1–9) and subsequently at the house of Ananias (Acts 9:10–16).

Patterns of response emerge from a comparative study of individual time lines. According to Clinton, at least twenty-five of these can be identified.

Four patterns may be classified as foundational, for they describe the backgrounds out of which leaders emerge. Three are transitional training patterns, which are connected with the move from one ministry phase to another through the course of a leader's life. Two testing patterns focus on faithfulness and character and two on discovering and using giftedness. According to Clinton, "The time of development of a leader depends upon response to processing. Rapid recognition and positive response to God's processing speeds up development. Slower recognition or negative response delays development."[48] Several later patterns describe various levels of maturity and effectiveness. A destiny pattern spans a leader's entire lifetime and enables a person to see his or her key contributions in full perspective.

As already noted, Clinton does not argue that all these elements are present in the formation of every leader or occur in the same sequence. Yet his approach identifies and correlates a wide range of experiences that many people have in their formation as leaders. It also demonstrates that biblical stories, as well as stories about leaders throughout history, provide material that can be used to determine frameworks, processes, and responses involved in leadership.

There is, however, a danger associated with this approach. It is sometimes difficult to resist finding what one is looking for in light of previous studies. It is also tempting to correlate these factors in ways that homogenize experiences or patterns too much. A related tendency is to abstract them too much from particular life settings or types of personalities. It is also easy to structure them in a sequence that is too fixed. In reading Clinton's work, the sheer number of process items, the abstract nature of his descriptive terms, and the systematizing of his leadership data lead to a sense that the organic and diverse character of leadership formation has been too tightly classified.

The biblical narratives reveal the highly individual—at times even idiosyncratic—way God leads and prepares people to fulfill his purposes. God's flexibility and versatility come through in story after story. The Holy Spirit—especially in the New Testament—also clearly has a role. Though Clinton affirms the role of the Spirit, at the practical level, his view does not leave enough room for the creative and diverse ways the Spirit works. At times there is something bureaucratic about Clinton's approach, which is influenced by the modern predilection with analyzing, classifying, and organizing all experience and training.

Also, many figures in the Bible worked mainly in the "secular" rather than the so-called religious sphere of life that Clinton examines. Some of these, such as political leaders or bureaucratic advisors, carried out their work in civic or community roles and institutions. Others engaged in various professions and trades. Examples include Joseph, a prime minister; Boaz, a city councilor; Bezalel and Oholiab, both master builders; Daniel, an exiled bureaucrat; Nehemiah, a city governor; Esther, a royal consort; and Priscilla and Aquila, tentmakers who were also engaged in mission. Notable here are the diverse ways in which these people were drawn to what God wanted them to do. Unlike the biblical figures Clinton examines, for example, prophets such as Isaiah (Isaiah 6) and Jeremiah (Jeremiah 1) or New Testament apostles such as Peter (John 21) and Paul (Acts 9), these people did not receive a direct call to a particular kind of work or position. They did not experience an unequivocal personal vision or call. Instead, they were drawn, guided, or led by God into the kind of position that would fulfill his purposes. Consider some examples from Robert Banks's *Faith Goes to Work: Reflections from the Marketplace.*

- Apart from his general dream of dominance over his brothers, Joseph experienced a succession of personal betrayals, reversals of fortune, periods out of public view, risky moral stands, delayed recognition, and unexpected calls upon his services. Through these events God gradually and providentially moved him into the high position where he could best serve the future of the nation of Israel (Genesis 37–41).

- On account of their expertise as master builders, Bezalel and Oholiab were recruited by Moses to build the tabernacle. In doing so, they assumed responsibility for a large number of volunteers from diverse crafts and trades (Exodus 35–38).

- Boaz came into his role as a progenitor of Christ by an unusual route. As a relative of the widowed Ruth, he accepted his obligation to marry her and to continue his kinsman's line (Ruth 1–4).

- Daniel, on account of his looks and aptitude, was required to undergo a course of study and training to become a civil servant. Aided by some

God-given academic and charismatic abilities, he was able to overcome a potentially unpopular moral course of action and ended up as the chief public servant in the land (Daniel 1–6).

- Esther, an exile, was drafted along with other young women into a beauty contest to see who would gain the king's hand in marriage. Because of her beauty and manner, she won, and through a series of risky and canny moves, she saved her people from genocide (Esther 1–9).
- Nehemiah, having retained a long-standing concern for his distant people and city, asked God for wisdom in finding a way back to them. As a reward for his service and reputation, the foreign rulers he served commissioned him to return and rebuild the city (Nehemiah 1–6).
- Priscilla and Aquila, a highly mobile and ethnically marginal couple, opened their home and offered work to a visiting apostle. This led to an invitation to travel with him and to engage in the work of church planting alongside their business of tentmaking (Acts 18–19).[49]

By diverse means God drew these people to the places where he wanted them to be and the tasks through which they could make the most significant contribution to his wider goals. The word *call* is often used in regard to such leading.

Related to this life-story approach are the findings from a survey of the life experiences of almost two hundred Lutheran CEOs conducted by William Diehl and presented in his book *In Search of Faithfulness: Lessons from the Christian Community*.[50] Diehl undertook this in response to Tom Peters and Robert Waterman's *In Search of Excellence: Lessons from America's Best-Run Companies*, which focuses on faithfulness rather than excellence as the dominant Christian goal.[51] Using various indicators of faithfulness such as spiritual growth and understanding, active prayer life, commitment to the community, financial stewardship, concern for ethics and justice, and simplicity of lifestyle, Diehl found that roughly 30 percent of the executives consistently scored higher than the others, sometimes by a factor of two or three. Endeavoring to find out what made the difference, he ran the data through his computer again and found only one common element. They all shared a sense of call, meaning they felt they were in the place God wanted them to be.

Although there are inadequacies in the life-story approach to leadership, it also broadens the biblical and theological framework for understanding leadership. While the trinitarian approach expands an understanding of leadership "upward" by seeking to integrate ideas based on the Godhead, the life-story approach expands an understanding "outward" by embracing the experiences of key figures among the people of God, past and present, who embody leadership through the Spirit's presence in their lives. This is a valuable contribution to the overall discussion of leadership.

Conclusion

An effective and comprehensive biblical theology of leadership must draw on the person and work of Christ, the nature and activity of the Trinity, and the way biblical figures were led by God to develop into effective coworkers with him. Paul's understanding and practice, as discussed earlier, should also be taken into consideration. It is also important to extend and supplement what we can learn from the Bible with other wise reflections and practices in the area of leadership, including approaches from a wide range of theological traditions. We need discernment to sort out what is true and false, fitting and inappropriate, abstract and practical, timely and outdated. The general presence of God's image in people, the general revelation of God's truth in the world—however limited or distorted it may sometimes be—and the general activity of the Spirit in life give us encouragement to do this. In the following chapters, this is what we seek to do.

3 Keys aspects of character
relating to leadership

practicing leader- ship through integrity, faithfulness, and service

Finding a valid starting point for reflecting Christianly on leadership is one challenge. Translating reflection into day-to-day working life is another. Doing so entails developing a comprehensive approach to leadership that involves the whole person and translating that approach into action. Attempts that seek to involve the whole person highlight the roles of imagination, emotion, intelligence, and character in those in leadership positions.

Toward More Holistic Leadership

In his book *Doing It Different: Lessons for the Imaginative Manager,* David Clutterbuck makes a plea that more attention be given to the catalytic role of the imagination in management.[1] Imagination makes a difference in how people see issues and tackle problems. It also involves creative behavior, which he describes as "walking around corners backwards." He sets out how effective use of imagination can make a contribution to such diverse aspects of an institution's life as having fun and dismantling inadequate parts of the organization. He also identifies the importance of the following: choosing from unlimited organizational shapes; generating a spirit of adventure; and the need to fight "normalization."[2]

Daniel Goleman, in his well-known books *Emotional Intelligence, Working with Emotional Intelligence,* and *Primal Leadership: Realizing the Power of Emotional Intelligence,*[3] declares that in addition to IQ, emotional intelligence, or s a critical role in work in general and leadership in particular. Indeed, intelligence, or a person's academic achievement, is only a reliable ... in 20 percent of cases of how effective a person will be in leadership. Since leadership in an organization is fundamentally about leading people, there is a need to understand them, relate to them, and draw the best out of them. Without emotional intelligence, other capacities a leader brings to the job, however highly developed, can be short-circuited.

Goleman goes on to describe the five key elements of emotional intelligence. Self-awareness, self-regulation, motivation, empathy, and social skills are all necessary for effective leadership. Expression of these, combined with what Goleman calls highly aware role mapping, that is, a perceptive understanding of the way people undertake their responsibilities in relation to those with whom they work, gives rise to what Carlos Raimundo describes as "relational capital."[4] This term describes the number of resources in an organization derived from the quality of human interactions in it. The presence or lack of relational resources is as much a factor in organizational growth and effectiveness as the presence or lack of financial resources.

At the same time, however, we should not minimize the importance of practical intelligence. Alistair Mant examined a number of exemplary leaders and discovered that they all exhibit a form of wisdom that is more than mere knowledge, even though they need relevant knowledge to operate effectively.[5] Such practical knowledge is broad rather than narrow. At its core is the ability to think systematically, to determine chains of cause and effect, and to understand the role of subsystems within larger systems. The outcome of such intelligence is timely judgment—the ability to size up a situation quickly and to act decisively.

At the heart of Mant's approach is what he calls ternary leadership. According to Mant, binary leadership focuses on direct leadership of a transactional kind that places interpersonal influence and persuasion at the center of relationships. As such, it is characterized by a fight/flight, win/lose, and power/survival way of operating. Ternary leadership is oriented more to transformation and can be either direct or indirect. In this model, relationships are governed by the purpose and object of the enterprise in which people are engaged, which demands more thought as well as a relational and consensual form of leadership. Failures in leadership frequently spring from a lack of practical intellectual firepower.[6]

Each of these aspects of leadership has a role to play in bridging the gap between aspiration and performance, but they tend to overlook a dimension of leadership without which efforts in these other areas are likely to fall short. This is the area of character. In philosophical discussions during the last two decades, several leading thinkers have contended that a focus on making ethical decisions contains a hidden assumption: Being able to work out what to do automatically involves possessing the ability to do it. Yet we cannot take this for granted. Christians recognize that, as a result of the fall, knowledge does not necessarily result in action. As Paul put it, "I have the desire to do good, but I cannot carry it out" (Rom. 7:18).

In recent years, several writers have highlighted the importance of character in the process of exercising leadership. In discussion with Peter Koestenbaum about his book *Leadership: The Inner Side of Greatness,*[7] Patricia La Barre argues that the basic defect in views of leadership today is the unimportance attached to the kinds of character-building conversations that open up the possibility for real change.

> The average person is stuck, lost, riveted by the objective domain. That's where our metrics are; that's where we look for solutions. It's the come-on of the consulting industry and the domain of all the books, magazines, and training programs out there. And that's why books and magazines that have numbers in their titles sell so well. We'll do anything to avoid facing the basic, underlying questions: How do we make truly difficult choices? How do we act when the risks seem overwhelming? How can we muster the guts to burn our bridges and to create a condition of no return?[8]

Good

People in leadership must be committed to grappling with what it takes to change deeply ingrained habits relating to how they think, what they value, how they manage frustration, and how they act. Here lies the zone of fundamental change and strength. As James Kouzes and Barry Posner have said, "Character counts!"[9]

Throughout the centuries, Aristotle's philosophical approach tended to be most influential in ethical reflection. This approach gave primary attention to how people gain the capacity to carry out their aspirations, determinations, and responsibilities. It focused on virtue ethics, that is, how to become the kind of person who would make the best choices, as opposed to decision ethics, that is, how to determine the most important factors that result in the best choices. In recent times, Alistair McIntyre has become the leading exponent of this approach to ethics among philosophers, while in theological circles, Protestant ethicists such as Stanley Hauerwas have developed a similar approach. So have some Catholic writers.[10] Parallel to this virtue-oriented approach is the character-centered approach of the wisdom writings in the Old Testament. While this religious tradition has not played as strong a role in recent discussions, its importance has been increasingly acknowledged in theological discussions of conduct. A focus on character, whether in philosophical or religious terms, recognizes that personal formation precedes as well as accompanies making good choices. Character not only gives a person a greater capacity to implement a decision but also shapes the kind of decision to be made. It has, therefore, both an informative as well as a performative contribution.

Since growth in character includes affective as well as volitional and cognitive development, it also affects a person's emotional intelligence and relational ability. It does this through generating a greater understanding within a leader of how he or she operates at these levels. Growth in character also helps a leader widen the frames of reference through which he or she seeks to understand how and why others react as they do and how better to work with and for them. Though character has less affect on a person's development of skills, it can assist the appropriateness and consistency with which a leader deploys those skills.

The discussion that follows focuses on three key aspects of character relating to leadership: faithfulness, integrity, and service.

Leadership and Faithfulness

As a leader, it is not enough simply to have faith or to be a person of faith in the workplace. That is, it is not enough just to believe privately certain core convictions or even to be publicly known as a Christian. Faithfulness is required as well as faith. Indeed, faithfulness is the concrete expression of faith in the workplace. Such faithfulness means more than maintaining a consistent personal relationship with God or talking about one's faith with others, operating in accord with the contractual agreement entered into on employment, or exhibiting loyalty to authority in the organization and encouraging others to do the same.

Faithfulness entails a closer and more far-reaching link between beliefs and behavior. Forging such a bridge requires a certain kind of character. For character to take root, people must first have principles, and principles must form into habits. From Robert Bellah's analysis of some *Habits of the Heart* to Stephen Covey's *Seven Habits of Highly Effective People,* there is greater recognition that inner priorities and values must be embodied in regular practices.[11] Many people in the workplace want leaders whose ways of operating are shaped not just by company policy, political correctness, or individualistic behavior but by character. Such an approach, however, does have some limitations.

- Too often it sounds as if developing the right kinds of principles and habits at work is simply a matter of working harder. Yet according to the New Testament, faith, and therefore faithfulness flowing from it, is more a gift to be requested than an achievement that is earned (see Eph. 2:8–9).

- The principles and habits discussed in most popular books do not go deep enough. Fairness, honesty, service, and excellence do not cover the full range of Christian qualities set out in the Bible (as in Gal. 5:22–23). For example, justice involves more than fairness, goodness more than honesty, sacrifice more than service, and faithfulness more than excellence.

- The principles outlined in some popular writings are too dry and abstract to motivate people to act faithfully. People require also the dispositions from which principled behavior flows. These develop largely through being on the receiving end of life-changing experiences and gratuitous acts of kindness that come through divine or human encounters—those that create personal transformation.

In the Bible, faithfulness is always concrete, never just an attitude or an ideal. The Bible acknowledges that because of the complexities of life, the application of faithfulness may vary according to circumstances. There are no simple answers or formulas for all occasions. Yet it is not enough for a person to have his or her heart in the right place. Faithfulness always involves practical decisions and actions.

Leaders must learn to live *out* as well as to live *by* faith, to *keep* as well as to *have* faith, and to be faith*ful* as well as to be *full* of faith. Such actions have advantages for both leaders and those in their organizations. Faithfulness leads to a clearer understanding of organizational goals and values, better morale, and a higher degree of trust. According to Max De Pree, "Trust grows when people see leaders translate their personal integrity into organizational fidelity," when followers see "that leaders can be depended on to do the right thing."[12] When leaders clearly and consistently express their faith through faithfulness in the workplace, they gain credibility. James Kouzes and Barry Posner claim that credibility is the cornerstone of effective leadership.[13]

Faithfulness also enhances the potential for growth in an organization. In for-profit organizations, faithfulness spills over into supplier and customer loyalty, greater cost advantage through superior productivity, and stronger and long-term investor commitment.[14] In nonprofit organizations, it creates greater buy-in of members, more vigorous initiative and effort, and more permanent financial support.

Faithfulness also has advantages for the wider community. An organization that models the way faithfulness can function increases trust in society and presents a model of organizational fidelity from which other institutions can learn. Faithfulness in action may also open up people to discovering the fundamental role of faith in life in general.

WITH RESPECT TO THE MISSION

Leaders who exhibit faithfulness have a clear sense of what they are doing and are able to deliver it. They either start or emerge in organizations that create value for employees and members, partners and allies, customers and clients. For example, stating a mission is an act of faith. A mission statement expresses a commitment to being as well as doing something. It is important for those in leadership positions, at any level, to be faithful to their organization's mission. What does this mean in practice?

First, they must continue to believe that what they have embarked on is achievable, and they must seek to operate in a way that is consistent with the content of the mission statement. This does not mean that when unanticipated difficulties or hurdles appear, they downplay them or pretend they do not exist. Rather, throughout, they maintain the viability of the mission and continue to uphold it, especially for those who are anxious. For example, Lee Iacocca's faith in the ultimate success of the faltering Chrysler Corporation was critical to restoring the confidence of a demoralized workforce and gaining financial support from the government.

Second, leaders should behave, relate, and operate in a way that reflects the character of the mission. If it puts customers first, they must put customers first. If it promises extraordinary service, they must provide the same. If it is committed to quality, they must create an environment that has this characteristic.

Third, leaders should seek to clarify in terms of the mission why they have adopted a certain process for decision making, devised a particular structure for change, or taken a specific course of action.

WITH RESPECT TO PROMISES

Over a period of time, leaders generally make promises to those who work with and for them. Unfortunately, there seems to be a growing disparity in both private and public life between the promises leaders make and the actions they take. Nowadays, most people seem to regard a promise as the expression of a hope rather than the creation of an obligation.

Because of the complexity and unpredictability of the marketplace, promises cannot always be kept, yet as far as possible, faithful leaders should seek to keep their word. They should not make contradictory promises to people inside and outside the organization. When they do so, questions soon arise about their integrity. They should also not make casual promises. Faithful leaders should seek to honor their promises despite altered circumstances.

WITH RESPECT TO MISTAKES

Like everyone, leaders make mistakes, but they are generally better at hiding them, protecting themselves from the consequences, or turning them to positive effect. Faithful leaders acknowledge their mistakes, seek to minimize future mistakes, and look for ways to learn the most from them. At the same time, they know that the future does not belong to those who make the least mistakes. In fact, they are aware that they need to encourage experimentation and innovation. When other people make mistakes, a leader who exhibits faithfulness holds people accountable for the mistakes but also forgives them and helps them to improve their performance.

In these days of job shift rather than job security, most organizations find it difficult to guarantee lifelong employment. How do leaders exercise faithfulness in such a climate? First, they can commit themselves to building or maintaining an organization that will last, despite the changes that take place. This may entail committing long-term to an organization and not pursuing better positions as they arise elsewhere. Such a leader can also seek to influence decisions that will enhance an organization's long-term capacity.

When he became CEO of Herman Miller, Max De Pree promised training for people who suffered from cutbacks to help make them more marketable, assisted them in finding new positions, and assured them of a salary until they received an offer comparable to their present positions. He showed a creative and responsible reformulation of the principle of loyalty.

There are other ways in which faithfulness can lead to loyalty. Leaders can provide organizational stability, share the profits, identify and empower the use of gifts, grant employees a sense of worth and a role in decision making, and give them incentives to come up with creative ideas from which they can derive a sense of genuine achievement. When these actions become standard operating procedures, then image and reality, ideals and practice, statements and behavior are merged, creating a stronger loyalty between employees and leaders.

Leadership and Integrity

On every side today we hear calls for greater integrity in personal, professional, and public life. But few pause to reflect for long on its full meaning, the complex challenges facing anyone who seeks to act with integrity, and what is involved in its everyday moment-by-moment practice. Occasionally, we have met people who have given the impression that integrity is a simple matter. One of us once spoke with a group of Christian civil servants about the appropriateness and legitimacy of connecting private values and public policy. A leading person in the group, who had been working in the attorney general's department for most of his life, said that in all his years of drafting legislation, he had not experienced a single moral challenge. He felt, therefore, that living with integrity was quite straightforward and did not require discussion.

On the other side are those who believe that, at least in certain occupations, integrity is impossible. In such cases, people must close their eyes to so much or make so many compromises that they cannot maintain ethical rectitude. Politics is one such occupation. Increasingly, law is another.

A recent handbook on business ethics written by Gordon Pearson argues for a position between these two extremes.[15] Pearson rejects what he regards as the unrealistic recommendations regarding organizational integrity in most writings on the subject and also the approach that sidelines ethical behavior. Arguing from Lawrence Kohlberg's stages of moral development from childhood to maturity, he accepts the less than normal ethical behavior and the lack of concern for social responsibility required in the early days of a business for it to survive and compete. The book therefore rules out attempts to operate in a thoroughgoing ethical way from the start through heroic individual efforts. Over time, however, an organization can adopt different standards that gradually attain higher levels of organizational integrity. While allowing that both leaders and organizations develop in their capacity to act with integrity, Pearson's equating of organizational and individual moral stages of development confuses categories and is therefore inadequate. The law rightly treats organizations as adult rather than infant or adolescent corporate selves. In addition, leaders in organizations are not at an infant-like level of moral and character development and should seek to elevate their understanding and behavior.[16]

There are, then, those who tend to be too naïve, those who tend to be too skeptical, and those who want to be neither but are in danger of defending less than appropriate behavior. The challenge is to recognize the insidious challenges to acting consistently with integrity and to endeavor to do so with a reasonable hope of attainment. As Christians, we acknowledge that at times our human frailty draws us off course and opens us up to failure. Though human frailty may make living with integrity difficult, it does not make it impossible.

What, however, do people mean when they call for greater integrity in the workplace? As Stephen Carter in his fine book on integrity says, "Everybody argues that the nation needs more of it . . . but hardly any of us stop to explain what we mean by it." "Indeed," he adds, "the only trouble with integrity is that everybody who uses the word seems to mean something slightly different."[17]

When the word *integrity* is used thoughtfully, it generally refers to a trait possessed by individuals who act in a principled way in difficult situations. For example, a doctor who does not bow to peer pressure to conceal the full facts about a colleague's harmful negligence, a lawyer who resists the temptation to shade the truth in defending someone, and a psychologist who refuses to treat clients as cases rather than as persons have integrity. Yet the word is also used in connection with groups and organizations, indicating that integrity can be a quality of a profession or a professional association. In this sense, the focus is on consistently acting in accordance with high moral standards and being willing to publicly defend those actions when they lead to controversy.

The word *integrity* also calls to mind certain related terms that come from the same root. The term *integral,* for example, speaks of what is inherent to, at the core of, a person. Having integrity is not the same as developing a certain skill. It refers to something more organic. Losing integrity does not just lead to having less of *something;* it means becoming less of a *someone.* "Integrity is not so much a virtue itself as a complex of virtues, the virtues working together to form a coherent character, an identifiable and trustworthy personality."[18]

As the related words *integrate* and *integration* show, integrity also involves consistency between the various parts of a person and his or her roles. Acting with integrity is more complex than simply fulfilling moral obligations. The question of standards, how to act rightly in one's work, involves more than asking, "What should I do?" in a particular situation. When integrity is present, there are no discrepancies between the way a person acts in one situation versus another or in one of their roles versus another. There is a consistency about all that a person does and a coherence in the way he or she carries out responsibilities. In a person of integrity, "there is a *togetherness* about his or her personality" that some might describe as "wholeness" and others as "holiness" of character.[19]

One indication of the renewed interest in integrity is the rise of professional ethics. Too often, however, professional ethics focuses on only moral principles without raising questions about the kind of character needed to implement them or the larger vision and mission that enlighten and motivate them. In professional ethics, decision making is also viewed too much as an individual affair, ignoring the need to consider the influence of the core institutional values and ethos that shape the dilemmas that individuals face. Discussion of professional ethics often takes place in an allegedly value-free context in which religious or ideological frameworks are excluded for the sake of inclusiveness. The trouble, then, is that the principles expounded do not have a ground of support that justifies their selection over that of others.

CHALLENGES FOR PROFESSIONALS

Some of the challenges that confront professionals are outlined by Donald Kraybill, Phyllis Pellman Good, and their coauthors in *Perils of Professionalism: Essays on Christian Faith and Professionalism*.[20] They include:

- serving the interest of a profession rather than the people it is designed to serve and rating accountability to it higher than accountability to them
- demonstrating the ability to create a professional service rather than meeting a demonstrable need in the community
- protecting the secrets of professional work rather than sharing them with clients so they can deal with certain problems themselves
- manufacturing a need that only a specialist can satisfy when there are simpler or more systematic ways of dealing with it
- overstepping one's position by performing services that exercise control rather than help the client
- using inside information gained professionally from a client to advance one's interests in some way

- abusing one's relationship with a client to gain sexual favors
- overcharging clients for services rendered

At the root of these bad choices in the workplace lie three factors: the flawed personalities of the people involved, intractable values or practices in organizations, and complex situations in which it is often difficult to discern what is really at stake.

What is at the heart of acting with moral integrity in any of these situations? One way to determine this is by considering the issue of integrity in the lives of biblical figures. Many could be studied from this angle, among them Joseph, Moses, Rahab, Samuel, David, Nehemiah, Jonah, and Daniel. Another way of approaching the issue of integrity is by asking the following questions:

- Will the action exhibit a proper regard for all the people involved, and will it exhibit a loving concern for them?
- Is it likely to lessen evil and extend justice, especially for those who are most vulnerable?
- In discussing the options, was a genuine concern for truth evident?
- Was there a recognition that a choice was involved and an avoidance of talk about "I had to do it"?
- Do both the process followed and the decision made display the virtue of patience?
- Can the decision be altered if circumstances change and another option opens up?

A SPECIFIC APPROACH

A contemporary approach to acting with integrity focuses on three connected perspectives, namely, an ethic of critique, of justice, and of care. The ethic of critique considers the distribution of power and privilege and who defines what is going on in a situation. In circumstances in which power and decision-making privilege are restricted to a few, it may be easier to compromise. The ethic of justice considers who may participate, how policies are determined, whether rights are involved and for whom, and by what criteria resources are allocated. This ethic invites a leader to consider issues of fairness and to invite participation in policy formation and resource allocation. The ethic of care concerns relationships and includes issues of dignity, human potential, and empowerment.[21]

Because Max De Pree committed himself to listening to the concerns of employees and created regular ways for this to happen, he was once asked why he didn't value adoptive births as much as natural births. He replied that he valued both equally. The female employee countered, "No, you don't. If you did you would offer the same benefits for adoptive births as for natural births." De Pree had assumed that company policy made no distinctions in this area. He changed the policy to provide equal resources for both situations.

This example points to the sharing of power between CEO and employee (ethic of critique), the value of the individual and the desire to improve her quality of life (ethic of care), and the changing of a policy so that all in the same situation could have access to the same resources (ethic of justice). When these three perspectives are used to balance and support decisions, the result is integrity.

In addition to using these perspectives, leaders can make decisions and act with integrity when they approach situations in the following ways: in a spirit of prayer, through which God may reveal fresh possibilities; with a willingness to consult with others in a vocational or communal group; and by aiming at a win-win rather than a win-lose situation.

The Role of Compromise

Though the opposite of integrity is often said to be compromise, the reality is not so simple. Compromise must not be confused with two processes that are at times intertwined with it. First, there is a difference between compromising and strategizing. The latter involves working out a long-term, often complex, set of tactics for reaching a desired end. This may involve moves and counter-moves, unexpected demands and apparent concessions that appear to obscure the goal of the exercise. Such strategies are a means to an end, temporary positions that are part of the larger exercise that is being played out, and may be good or bad. Second, compromising is not the same as negotiating. There are legitimate and illegitimate ways of negotiating, but compromise is not necessarily involved in them.

What, then, is compromise? Mostly the word has a negative connotation. For example, it can be used to describe a decision or an action that entails a lowering of standards either on the grounds of expediency or to relieve pressure. When persons fail to act with consistency, they are said to have "compromised their integrity." To make or accept a compromise is to cross a moral line and therefore betray one's core convictions. Yet the word can also be used in a positive way, as when we talk about making "a good compromise." This may involve finding a middle ground between two options based on different principles or the same principle.

Life is full of situations in which it is not possible to do what one wants. Such is the case with politics, which is often described as "the art of compromise." In the world of commerce, compromise when making business deals is also accepted. In such fields, resources, supplies, time, and personnel are often in short supply, and choices have to be made about who will receive them. People may have deeply held conflicting opinions, and it is only through trade-offs that decisions can be reached.

A case can be made for legitimate compromise by examining the many biblical stories in which it is encouraged. A classic example is that of Naaman, the advisor to a foreign king who on a visit to Israel was healed by a leading prophet of the day. Because of the difficulty he faced as the lone believer in a foreign culture, he was permitted to bow his head in an act of pagan worship when he returned to his own country so long as he continued to give his allegiance to the true God (2 Kings 5:15–19).

Another example is the meeting of Paul and Barnabas with the apostles and elders in Jerusalem to discuss the validity of the Gentile mission. If Greek and Roman converts would agree to avoid certain actions that Jewish Christians found offensive (Acts 15:23–29), then the latter would endorse Paul's initiative without requiring Greek and Roman believers to be circumcised.

An interesting study is Paul's apparently contradictory practice of circumcising one of his coworkers, the half-Jew Timothy, but not another, the Greek Titus. His actions reflected his stated practice of becoming "all things to all men so that by all possible means I might save some" (1 Cor. 9:22). He adjusted his practice in light of people's sensitivities in order to give them unhindered access to what was most important. At the same time, he would not move an inch when he felt that doing so would jeopardize a central Christian truth. For example, he disagreed with Peter at Antioch when he encountered what he considered a betrayal of basic gospel principles (Gal. 2:11–14).

Biblical stories touch our imaginations as well as our minds and evoke a range of possible applications. Yet not only stories but also biblical metaphors, images, symbols, and models can help us understand appropriate compromise. The biblical metaphors "salt" and "light" are guides to how God's people are called to operate. Other images relate to God's people being "aliens and strangers" yet also a "royal priesthood" among others in the world. There is also the powerful symbol of God's people "taking up the cross" daily in the workplace. We must be careful, however, not to straitjacket these metaphors, images, and symbols into a moral framework that is not large enough for them. If we think only in terms of black and white, good and bad, right and wrong, we miss the profound gospel content of these biblical features and risk hindering ourselves from making positive compromises when they are morally necessary.

In Proverbs and other Old Testament wisdom writings, decisions are frequently judged by whether they are wise or unwise, fitting or unfitting, appropriate or inappropriate. For example, when a person is in the presence of a superior who is at times hostile, what is appropriate is not simply a matter of whether what one says is true or false but whether it is a good time to speak or how much should be revealed and in what way (Eccles. 8:2–6). There are times when it is better not to press for something that is good simply because it would bring about an unproductive reaction. On other occasions, it may be best to wait for a more opportune time. In some cases, it is wise to engage in an action even if it is not what we would most prefer, for it may be the best that is likely to come out of the situation.

If such a decision is the best decision in a particular situation, is it not then the will of God for us then and there, even though we may feel we should do more? For example, when Jesus was unable to heal in a certain place because the people's faith was lacking, it was not a negative compromise on his part for which he required forgiveness. If, for reasons beyond our control, we have to choose between helping one person properly and two poorly, what more can we do and what do we have to confess? If we have only a limited amount of time or number of resources, our options are limited. We may and probably should experience regret, but is more than that appropriate? Helpful here is Dietrich Bonhoeffer's distinction between ultimate (that is, "ideal world") and penultimate (that is, "real world") realities, the latter constrained by events, situations, and people in the world. Sometimes, as he says, the constraints we operate under require us to "sacrifice a fruitless principle to a fruitful compromise."[22] In other words, we will achieve more by maximizing what is possible, even if it is not all we would like to do, than by holding out for an ideal that is incapable of realization.

To make compromises that have integrity, leaders should have the following in view:

- Because behavior flows from a sense of who they are and where they are heading, they should have a profound grasp of the way God shares his character and purposes with those who are his, as shown in the Bible.
- They should be aware of how their own life stories fit into the central and still ongoing purposes of God and allow them to be shaped by guiding images, metaphors, and stories in the Bible as well as basic beliefs and principles in it.
- Since good compromises are more a product of good character than good decision-making capacities, they should continue to give priority to character in their life journeys.
- To have a proper perspective of the particular issue at hand, they should keep the big vocational picture in mind, never letting go of their basic aims and purposes.

Leadership and Service

A Seminal Discussion of Servanthood

Robert Greenleaf, during his time as a manager at AT&T, introduced the idea of servanthood into the discussion of leadership. A Quaker by background,

Greenleaf, at a critical point in his life, encountered the writings of the famous German novelist Herman Hesse. Especially influential on Greenleaf was a story in Hesse's novel *Journey to the East*.[23] This story, influenced by Eastern thought, gave Greenleaf the idea of the servant as leader. In his writings, however, this idea is placed in a broader Christian, specifically Quaker, framework.[24]

While Greenleaf occasionally refers to the presence of servant leader motifs in the lives of such figures as Lao Tzu, Buddha, and Confucius, he mainly draws attention to the fact that "the idea of servant is deep in our Judeo-Christian heritage. Servant (along with serve and service) appears in the Bible more than thirteen hundred times."[25] Greenleaf did not have any formal theological or ethical training, but as Anne Fraker comments, "He developed a sense of ethics from his own Judeo-Christian upbringing and later Quaker affiliation," as well as through his workplace experiences and meditation.[26] Others also acknowledge "the importance of Quaker values in shaping [his] orientation."[27]

While he does not often explicitly mention Jesus, Greenleaf regards him as the archetypal leader, focusing primarily on Jesus' distinctive teaching and behavior. Some of Greenleaf's favorite stories are of Jesus washing his disciples' feet and Jesus' encounter with the woman who had committed adultery.[28] Jesus as a sensitive, moral, and compassionate leader particularly catches his attention. For Greenleaf, Jesus' inspired and creative contribution was obscured by the codifying and co-opting work of the church in subsequent centuries.[29] The early Protestant Reformers and their more radical Anabaptist counterparts removed some of the accretions and enabled us to see the original Jesus again. Although Greenleaf regards Quaker leaders such as George Fox and John Woolman as operating in a spirit similar to that of Jesus, he is also critical of them for failing to develop an adequate structure for "a society of equals in which there is a strong lay leadership."[30]

Greenleaf advocates the relevance of servant leadership for the marketplace, not just the church. This runs counter to the power-seeking, take charge, command, and control stance so commonly associated with leadership. For him, servant leadership means serving others and placing the good of others and the organization over the leader's self-interest. While this contradicts the abuse of power, such leadership does not avoid the exercise of power or influence. Servant leadership is not a kind of anti-leadership, for leading takes place through foresight, courageous action, and accountability, even though such actions take place in the context of shared decision making and are exercised among rather than over others.

From Greenleaf's writings, Larry Spears has identified the following critical characteristics of servant leadership: the ability to listen to others and discern the will of a group, to have empathy, to help make both others and oneself whole, to rely on persuasion rather than coercion and positional authority, to think and act beyond day-to-day realities, to hold in trust and be a good steward of an institution, and to build community among one's colleagues and fellow workers. These characteristics, however, are by no means exhaustive.[31] In his list of key working principles of servant leadership, Walter Wright—influenced by both Greenleaf and Max De Pree—notes that leadership is about influence and service, vision and hope, character and trust, relationships and power, and dependency and account-ability.[32] Some adherents to servant leadership stress its compatibility with proper accountability, creative rather than disruptive conflict, and tough caring.

THE LATER VARIANT OF STEWARDSHIP

A more recent variation of the servant leadership model is one revolving around stewardship and developed by Peter Block, building on his earlier work titled *The Empowered Manager*.[33] As shown in the subtitle of his *Stewardship: Choosing Service over Self-Interest*, the idea of service is central to his approach.[34] For Block, stewardship is the "umbrella idea" for achieving change in the way institutions are governed, especially in the challenging areas of the distribution of power, purpose, and rewards. This goes beyond more technical fix-it style programs by highlight-ing the need for people to see their role as primarily that of a trustee of something valuable who passes it on to the next generation with added value. Stewardship "is the willingness to be accountable for the well-being of the larger organization by operating in service, rather than control, of those around us."[35] This runs counter to the attitude of self-interest that so often drives leaders.

Block's preference is to retire the language of leadership in favor of the lan-guage of stewardship. Doing so involves moving from patriarchy to partnership and from security to adventure. To achieve this, leaders must move beyond dominance and the wish for dependency and be willing to make full disclosure and develop more open and inclusive managerial practices, offer choice to and build capability among employees, and build widespread financial account-ability throughout the organization. This results in the creation of a balance rather than a hierarchy of power within an organization, a commitment to the entire community rather than to individuals or teams, empowerment of all to help define the organization's purpose and ethos, and an equitable rather than an unbalanced distribution of rewards. The ultimate test of the effectiveness of such an approach is whether it passes the test of the marketplace but continues to incorporate the concerns of the Spirit.

As Block suggests, putting an emphasis on service and stewardship would result in "the end of the era of leaders" but "would not eliminate leaders."[36] People would still function in significant roles and positions, but they would operate from among rather than over others, seek participation more than make a presentation, establish connections before expressing content, and ask ques-tions as much as give answers. They would also recognize that change emerges as people are encouraged to make unique contributions and as conversations take place within various parts and levels of an organization.

Though this view has been criticized for being otherworldly and not facing the hard realities of life in the marketplace, companies that have adopted this philosophy of servant leadership have done extremely well. Among them are Herman Miller, ServiceMaster, and TD Industries, all of whom have been featured in lists of highly profitable corporations and the best companies to work for. Still, this model has limitations and difficulties at both the religious and the practical level.

Greenleaf focuses on Jesus as a moral example, falling under the critique of Ken Blanchard, who says that "when people talk about servant-leadership, Jesus is often a model, without even referring to this ultimate sacrifice."[37] And while Greenleaf places a strong emphasis on the Spirit at times—as in his remark that the "Spirit is the driving force behind the motive to serve"[38]—he tends to place too little stress on the specific content of the Spirit's character and role. This might also explain the more generic rather than specifically Christian references to the Spirit sometimes given in his work.[39] This is probably a result of the Quaker emphasis on "the inner Spirit" or the influence of Hesse's mystical interests. Advocates of servant leadership have sometimes quoted Jewish mystics and Buddhist masters as well as Jesus and the prophets.

For some people in leadership positions, the language of servanthood has negative connotations. As Shirley Roels has pointed out, servanthood is sometimes understood in terms of overly self-effacing and other-determined ways of operating. These have more to do with servitude than with service. The word is particularly open to abuse when applied to those in a position of disadvantage or forced inequality, such as many women and minority groups. In these cases, the word does not retain its biblical sense: The status of servants was based on the positions and responsibilities of the people they served. Gone, then, are the loftier biblical overtones of being a servant of the One who is above all others, namely, God, and of having the responsibility of keeping his purposes and ways of operating firmly in view in any position or work.[40]

Though Greenleaf insists that a leader is a servant first and only in the wake of that service is a leader, many people in authority place the main emphasis on the second word rather than on the first. In their dealings with others, they may be more approachable, but they still retain close control of what happens, supervise most of what takes place, and reserve the right to make basic decisions on their own. Ultimately, they operate in ways that are not much different from those of traditional leaders. Such people have co-opted the language of servant leadership for their own agendas and purposes. Sad to say, this has often been the case in the church and in many religious organizations.

Overall, the word *servanthood* is in danger of being viewed through the distorting lens of its contemporary misuse by those in authority. It is also in danger of being viewed too little in terms of its full Christian meaning. The trouble with the phrase "servant leadership," therefore, is that though it moves away from inadequate views of leading others, it still gets the order of the words wrong.

Leadership is the key term, and *servant* is the qualifier. What we need today are not, as is so often suggested, more *servant leaders* but, properly understood, more *leading servants*. We need people who will serve the mission, structures, and members of an organization in a way that goes beyond their peers and points the way forward for others.

It is not always easy to work out how to make the notion of servanthood operational in organizations. Too often the call to be a servant has an idealistic ring about it that does not sit well with the practicalities and compromises of so much daily work. Yet clues to what it entails are evident. One can look at the contribution of those in an organization who are regarded as its most appreciated servants. It can be seen in those who do not delegate to others what they can do themselves. It can be seen in an unwillingness to delegate difficult matters and the willingness to take full responsibility for them. Servanthood is evident in those who depend on others for wisdom instead of relying on their own resources, those who take a stand on matters even at the cost of their positions, those who are willing to suffer voluntary loss for their organization.

Some years ago, one of us visited a monthly breakfast attended by twenty-five Christian businesspeople from a range of churches. After eating, it was their custom for a member of the group to explain a pressure or difficulty in his or her work. On this particular day, the case in question revolved around the issue of mandatory downsizing. The senior manager presenting the case had to fire one of his two assistants. Both were highly competent associates. One had more experience and had been with the company longer. The other was going through a time of marital stress and personal loss of confidence and was not performing as well. The presenter felt that seniority should probably be the prime consideration. Yet he also sensed that firing the junior assistant would put that person's marriage and self-esteem under even greater stress.

Discussion continued for some time, and as the breakfast drew to a close, the presenter said that as a result of the group's deliberations, he had a growing sense that he should keep both assistants, promote the senior assistant to his own position, and fire himself. This was a striking example of someone who was willing to sacrifice himself for the sake of his colleagues.

Such an approach to leadership is applicable not only to those at the top of an organization. It can take place at any level. Especially significant, however, are the abilities to faithfully articulate, embody, and extend the mission of the organization and to draw in and empower others to implement and enhance it.

Conclusion

The aspects of faithfulness, integrity, and service discussed in this chapter are most perfectly embodied in Jesus, the ultimate role model not only for life but also for leadership (Heb. 12:2–3). This fact highlights two things. First, leadership is about who a person is before and alongside what he or she does. It grows out of personal wholeness as well as wholeness in the sense of breadth and balance of life. Such wholeness is not so much a quality or a mark of leadership as a precondition and a catalyst for it. Only by possessing it can people avoid the intrusion and the effects of the shadow side of leadership. These include always needing to be in charge and have everything under control, inflicting pathology and inadequacies on others, falling into the messiah trap with its attendant danger of workaholism, becoming a mere persona rather than a genuine person, and failing to overcome the inability to share weakness or face failure. Second, because leadership is ultimately about who a person is as a whole, it is fundamentally about followership before it is about leadership. It is only through the gift on the cross of Jesus' life and the gift of the Spirit that people have any chance of developing into the kinds of people who have the capacity to serve and therefore lead others well.

Eugene Petersen catches the flavor of these two points when he writes:

> Leaders influence followers far more by the context out of which they live—body language, personal values, social relationships, dress, consumer choices, chosen companions—than the text they articulate. Leadership is not primarily a skill, although it employs skills. Leadership is a way of living that suffuses everything we do and are. Leadership is a way of being in the family and marriage, a way of being among friends, a way of going to work, a way of climbing mountains, but most basic, a way of following Jesus. And so in a culture in which there is an enormous attention to leadership, it is essential that we take a long hard look at what is previous and foundational to leadership, namely, "followership"—following Jesus (Mark 1:17). *Followership* gets us moving obediently in a way of life that is visible and audible in Jesus, a way of speaking, thinking, imagining, and praying that is congruent with immediate realities of "kingdom" living. Following enters into a way of life that is given its character and shape by *the* leader. Following involves picking up rhythms and ways of doing things that are mostly unsaid. Following means that you can't separate what the leader is doing and the way she or he is doing it. For those of us who are in positions of leadership—as parents, teachers, pastors, employers, physicians, lawyers, homemakers, students, farmers, writers—our following skills take priority over our leadership skills. Leadership that is not well-grounded in *followership*—following Jesus—is dangerous to both the church and the world.[41]

Frank
Soren
Janet
Gordon

leadership style predominant - what do you know of leader style evident in person approach
In what ways or in what situation is one style(s) evident?
Impact of worldview have to on style

christian leadership in action

Some Exemplary Case Studies

This concluding chapter looks at a number of significant figures who exemplify different facets of Christian leadership and in the process challenges some common assumptions about what leadership in general involves.

Are Leaders Always Ahead of Those around Them?

According to most writers on the subject of leadership, one mark of leaders is that they are always out in front of others—their colleagues, subordinates, and competitors. Leaders are not *above* others as much as *ahead* of others. Linguistically, this is what "taking the lead" means. Being ahead of others can take many different forms, such as discerning a need that cries out to be met, identifying business trends before anyone else, experimenting with new methods and approaches to familiar challenges, undertaking creative research and development, forming and heading a pioneering enterprise, creating innovative structures and delivery systems, or finding new ways of adding value to a product or a service.

All things being equal, success is said to come to the person, group, or organization that is able to get ahead of others in any of these ways. Even if circumstances require a temporary halt, stepping sideways to move forward, or a strategic retreat to rethink priorities, leaders are the first ones to realize the necessity for such a move. They may consult with others before deciding what to do and may seek others' help in explaining proposed changes, but in and through all of this, what marks leaders is their knack for seeing things in advance of others and staying ahead of the pack. While this quality is a part of what leadership involves, it is not always necessary for good leadership. Indeed, it is sometimes more important for leaders to be behind rather than in front of those around them.

FRANK BUCHMAN: A LEADER OF A GLOBAL MOVEMENT

Frank Buchman was born in 1878 in a small pietistic Lutheran town in Pennsylvania. His family later moved to the nearby burgeoning city of Allentown. After assisting in a church in a mixed neighborhood in Philadelphia, Buchman, around the age of thirty, became the YMCA secretary at Pennsylvania State College. Over the next five years, he had a significant religious influence there, and his gifts in communicating and organizing became known to college ministers around the country. He was offered a teaching post at Hartford Theological Seminary and from there undertook several speaking tours in Asia. Though when speaking he was sometimes prone to self-advertisement, from early on he looked for ways to bring others into the limelight while he stood by and supported them from behind. As one observer commented at the time, "I have been interested in watching this man Buchman all day. He is always in the background, pushing others into places of leadership and responsibility." According to his biographer, while he was "an ardent advertiser of his own activities, he was also surprisingly self-effacing. . . . Extrovert in his manner, he was at heart profoundly reserved."[1]

Through his travels, Buchman had a growing sense that God was calling him "to remake the world" through encouraging dramatic personal change in the lives of key individuals. He had already begun to display an unusual gift for personal relationships, especially with people of a higher social standing or in significant positions of responsibility. Realizing that this task was too large for a heroic-type leader, he began enlisting a diverse group of people to join him. By his early forties, he had drawn together a number of inexperienced but dedicated people from America and Britain who were willing to travel as teams to colleges and other institutions. Wherever they went, these teams gathered people together for several days in a relaxed atmosphere to consider fundamental life decisions. After two years of coordinating such teams, Buchman resigned his position at Hartford, the last paid position he would ever have, and threw himself into what would become his life work.

What he started contained the seeds of what became known in the late 1920s as the Oxford Movement and a decade later as Moral Re-Armament. His declared aim was to change leaders and to create the leadership that will alter present conditions. This led him into an unceasing itinerant life, one that was nurtured and guided by his practice of waiting on and listening to God for an hour each morning. As the work grew, he became increasingly aware that people were attracted to events by the quality of the team members rather than by his personal presence with them for a limited time. He decided, therefore, to create and train a highly disciplined team that would remain together for a longer period of time. In time, this original group multiplied, and with his encouragement, individual teams began visiting other countries. As he entered his fifties, Buchman shifted his focus to preparing new team members for this expanding work. He always felt it was better to give time offstage to ten people who would do the work than to try and do it center stage himself.

During the 1930s, as international conflicts intensified and the specter of war threatened, Buchman concentrated his efforts on encouraging peace among national leaders. He and his teams worked hard in Europe to prevent the growth of Nazism and after World War II sought to bring conflict resolution to troubled and volatile situations. Because all these efforts took place behind the scenes, they rarely received attention in the media. Outsiders frequently viewed Buchman's activities as secretive and sectarian and consequently often criticized or opposed it. These developments led Buchman to move even farther into the background. It is a testimony to his approach that after his death in the early 1960s, the movement continued to operate through the exercise of collective rather than single leadership.

The tantalizing question about Buchman is this: Without binding anyone by a vow, contract, or financial guarantee, how did he gather so many diverse full-time and part-time colleagues who worked with him during his lifetime and continued to work with one another after his death? Even after observing him for ten years, Arnold Lunn, the well-known author and one-time critic of Buchman, failed to find a satisfactory answer: "He has no charisma that I can see. He isn't good-looking, he is no orator, he has never written a book, and he seldom even leads a meeting. Yet statesmen and great intellects come from all over the world to consult him, and a lot of intelligent people have stuck with him, full-time without salary, for forty years, when they could have been making careers for themselves. Why?"[2] Henry van Dusen concluded that the answer lay partly in his pre-vision, his understanding of human nature, and his confidence in his method of working. But above all, it lay in "the absolute deliverance of self—his hopes, his necessities, his reputation, his success—into the direction of the Divine Intention."[3]

In other words, it was primarily his focus on, or his abandonment to, what he perceived as God's work that was decisive.[4] "I had nothing to do with it," he once said. "I only obey and do what He says."[5] This meant, of course, that he was often the first to see what needed to be done and to test it. Those attracted to his movement were encouraged to emulate his actions rather than simply fall in behind him. Convinced that "he was wonderfully led to those who were ready" for this challenge, he believed that they were capable under God of more than they realized. He did not feel that he had any ability that others could not experience themselves. His operating principle was to "accept people at any point at which they are willing to arrive, and not urge them to do anything they are not led to do." Otherwise, he said, "I should be surrounded by a group of parasites rather than people who are taught to rely on God and let Him direct them individually."[6] Despite his pivotal role in the movement, Buchman viewed leadership as "the task of the whole fellowship."[7]

IMPLICATIONS

Leaders who place themselves behind others do not just give others room to take the lead but also personally back them as they do so and provide whatever resources—material, financial, and institutional—they need to succeed. Some cultures understand the importance of this dual way of operating better than others. One summer a few years ago, Robert and his wife were driving north over the border into British Columbia. On a high mountain pass, they stopped at a gas station to refuel. The station also housed a restaurant and a small museum. Inside the museum, which was a simple one-room affair, were artifacts, pictures, documents, and stories associated with the local Indian tribe. One of the stories caught his eye.

A member of the tribe had become separated from it. He looked everywhere for tracks but could not find them. In the course of his wanderings, he came across an Indian from a neighboring tribe. After they greeted each other and caught up on local news, he asked the following questions:

"Have you seen my people?"
"How many of them were there?"
"When was this?"
"Where were they?"
"In which direction were they headed?"
"How fast were they going?"

Much to his relief, the wandering tribesman received the answers he was seeking. After thanking his informant, he said, "I must find them—I am their *leader!*"

The most interesting aspect of this story is that it reveals how great a leader this man was. He had trained the members of his tribe so well that they had left him behind. Though it is right and proper for leaders at times to be ahead of those around them, at other times it is just as important for them to be behind them. They can do this by actively promoting and supporting people so they can make the best contribution possible. Leaders who are preoccupied with being out in front are in danger of neglecting this responsibility. Then they wonder why their people find it so difficult to keep up with them. When leaders give others the backing they need to develop, it is not long before some of their protégés begin to outdistance them in certain areas. When this happens, leaders find themselves behind those around them in another way. Yet this should not cause them alarm but deep satisfaction, for it frees them to move ahead into new areas, leaving those they have trained in charge of what they have left behind.

Does a Leader Need a Certain Kind of Personality?

Many organizations have an ideal type of leader in mind. The ideal often has to do with experience, abilities, and skills. But often, consciously or unconsciously, there is a preferred personality. This may be based on the character of an earlier leader who was greatly admired, a leader in another organization who is considered the best in the field, or the typical characteristics of a leader according to the training programs members of the organization have attended. A notion of an ideal type of leader also appears in connection with particular occupations. The top businesspeople are tough, social workers are caring, lawyers are hardheaded, salespeople are aggressive, accountants are unemotional, and psychologists are sensitive. Sometimes it is possible to choose between two types that are equally acceptable: Teachers may be strict or sympathetic, judges may be grave or acerbic, artists may be soulful or flamboyant.

People also have expectations about the kind of personality leaders should have when their roles involve a high degree of public visibility, as in civic or political life. Such people should be confident and assured. They should be willing to engage in self-presentation and promotion. They should be significantly motivated by self-advancement and fulfillment.

Overall, it is widely believed that there is a general correlation between personality and position. That fit may differ from occupation to occupation, from organization to organization, and from culture to culture. It may be flexible rather than tight, allowing for a range of possibilities or variations. It may vary according to the changing nature of an occupation, organization, or culture. It may depend on the degree to which the person or institution concerned is going through a critical phase. But there is still an inclination to believe that certain types of personality mesh better with certain types of positions.

We are not suggesting that personality and position have nothing to do with each other. What we want to challenge is the assumption that there must be a consistent and significant relationship between the two for good leadership to take place. In the end, a good match depends on what a particular situation demands.

SØREN KIERKEGAARD: A PUBLIC INTELLECTUAL

Søren Kierkegaard was born in 1813 to bourgeois parents in Copenhagen. He suffered from a curvature of the spine that left him with a permanent stoop.

This gave him, according to some contemporaries, "a gnome-like appearance." But it was clear from an early age that he was extremely intelligent and psychologically observant. He developed into a gifted conversationalist and had, on occasion, a sarcastic wit. These gifts soon made him well known to the intellectual and literary society in Copenhagen, though he preferred the company of friends, ordinary folk, and children.

In his early twenties, Kierkegaard's first articles appeared in newspapers. This was during a period when he turned his back on Christianity. In his twenty-fourth year, however, he committed himself fully to God and resumed study for a master's degree in theology. After a deeply romantic attachment to a young woman, Kierkegaard suddenly broke off the engagement, causing a furor among social circles in the city. In 1843, at age thirty, his first major work, *Either/Or,* was published under a pseudonym. It represented his journey from an aesthetic to an ethical stance toward life and was a literary sensation in Copenhagen. Two more personal works immediately followed (*Repetition* and *Fear and Trembling),* spurred in part by his doomed love affair. In these and the books that followed, Kierkegaard led his readers beyond aesthetic and ethical approaches to life to one that was overtly religious.

His next publication, *Philosophical Fragments,* indirectly asked, "What is Christianity?" and "How does one become a Christian?" Another book (*The Concept of Dread)* probed in a profoundly psychological way the nature of original sin. A year later, the last of his pseudonymous writings, *Stages on Life's Way,* continued the account of his spiritual journey. This was followed by his greatest work, *Concluding Unscientific Postscript to the Philosophical Fragments.* During this prolific four-year period, Kierkegaard found his vocation as a writer and, in addition to the works mentioned, composed seven volumes of what he called "edifying discourses," thoughtful devotional reflections on what was involved with being a Christian. Since, as a layman, he could not preach from the pulpit, he used books to communicate with a wider audience.

In the late 1840s, Kierkegaard was criticized as a writer in a weekly scandal sheet called *The Corsair.* Though he was not named outright, highly insulting cartoons made it clear that he was the object of attack. The criticism was directed at his motives and character as well as his writings and continued for the best part of a year. Other papers followed suit, and as a result, Kierkegaard could not appear in public without facing ridicule from even the ordinary citizens of the city. He was pilloried as both a pathetic egotist and a comic figure, the village idiot of Copenhagen. He was even featured as the main character in a successful farce that played in theaters all over Denmark. Only once did he issue a public reply, and then he lapsed into silence. With this, all hope of his having a significant impact as a writer was gone. Even the name Søren, the most common name in the country, fell into disfavor.

In spite of everything, Kierkegaard learned to view these events as part of God's plan for his life, and he remained convinced of his vocation as a writer. He began to come to terms with being a prophet who was misunderstood, not only among the literati but also by the general population. Unexpectedly, the king of Denmark continued to seek his advice during the time of public attack and even offered him an annual gratuity to cover publication expenses. Kierkegaard politely refused, stating his need to maintain independence and to demonstrate that his only allegiance was to God. When, in his thirty-fourth year, he began writing his devotional trilogy (*Edifying Discourses, Works of Love,* and *Christian Discourses*), he laid aside all attempts to speak indirectly about Christ, a step that was strengthened by a deep spiritual experience that he described as a kind of "second conversion."

While he continued to produce devotional works, in his late thirties, he focused especially on the complacency and superficiality of conventional Christianity. A critique of institutional Christianity had been implicit in his writings for some time. Now, in a trilogy (*The Sickness unto Death, Training in Christianity,* and *For Self-Examination*), this came to the forefront. In the first, he accused the church of giving people religious tranquilizers rather than helping them to undergo radical surgery. In the second, he criticized it for obscuring the genuine character of Christianity and making it too easy to be a believer. (Instead of converting pagans to Christianity, he said, Christianity had itself become a form of paganism.) In the third, he attacked the church for objectifying the Word of God so much that people were relieved of the obligation to make it personal and live it out. He held back half of this volume from publication lest it bring pain to the primate of the state church, Bishop Mynster, one of the church's better leaders and role models who had also been his father's pastor.

Because of their small readership, these books stirred up little reaction. Initially, Kierkegaard did not mind, but after a time he felt the need to take a more public stance. Though he would have preferred to remain in the background, he experienced an inner compulsion that would not go away. He knew that to speak out would break not only his own heart but those of various people dear to him, including the bishop. He knew that ultimately he had no choice and had to call institutional religion what it was, a Sunday religion that was neither rooted deeply enough in the soul nor applied radically enough to daily life. Even after Bishop Mynster died, in deference to his theological teacher's desire to become the bishop's successor, he waited almost twelve months before he spoke out. In 1854, he wrote twenty articles in a journal, *The Fatherland,* and continued the attack in nine editions of his own periodical, *The Instant* (now gathered together under the title *Attack upon Christendom*). Many of these critiques focused on the compromised position of the clergy as salaried functionaries of the state. For him, the idea of a Christian nation, indeed, of Christendom itself, was a betrayal of the gospel.

Kierkegaard found himself at the center of an acrimonious public controversy. Though the clergy bitterly opposed him, this time the common people responded to his message. All of a sudden he was popular again, and even some of his earlier books began to sell. He was uncomfortable with his newfound celebrity status. It was something he had neither anticipated nor desired. As John Gates says, Kierkegaard regarded himself "not as a reformer, but as a detective ferreting out the evidence." He was simply trying to tell the truth, not become the center of a public controversy surrounded by admirers or detractors.[8] He did not feel equipped to handle the pressure this created, the misunderstanding it involved, and the abuse it generated.

Some people find themselves at home in the glare of publicity. They even warm to the prospect of battle. Instead of feeling overwhelmed by criticism and ridicule, they are motivated by them into even greater efforts. For Kierkegaard, however, the more combative the discussion became, the more he wanted to stay in the background. Though he worked hard at relating to others socially and could be a congenial and stimulating companion, he was essentially a private, introspective, and sensitive person. If God wanted him to operate in the limelight, why had he not been given the temperament to do so? By nature he was retiring and nonconfrontational. Why had God placed him in this position? Why not someone who was better suited to the task?

But the more Kierkegaard pondered his situation, the more he began to see a divine logic to it. While, from one angle, it made sense to place in the public spotlight someone who was constitutionally equipped to deal with it, from another, doing so involved a greater risk. Such a person would be more vulnerable to the temptations of public life. He would be more likely to allow his public position, or the public attention he received, to go to his head. A more private person is largely protected from these temptations, preferring to withdraw from the limelight, not get lost in it, and more likely to fall into self-doubt than into vanity. What appeared at first sight to be a mismatch of personality and position, therefore, made sense as long as the person in question possessed other abilities—sharpness of mind, a passion for truth, and a capacity to communicate—to undertake the task.

Kierkegaard died as he was preparing the final *Instant* for publication. He was only forty-two years old. While his work had limited influence during his lifetime, almost a century later his writings became available to a wider audience and began to receive their full due. Since then he has had a major impact on a continuing line of novelists, intellectuals, philosophers, and theologians, not to mention a wide range of thoughtful people who have read his works.

IMPLICATIONS

In these days of pervasive personality tests, we need to be especially careful not to tie a particular personality too closely to a specific task, occupation, or position. Such tests do reveal factors that should be taken into consideration, but these factors should not be determinative. There is always the danger of introducing inadequate cultural assumptions into an assessment of what a person can or should do.

Theological considerations must also be taken into account. On the one hand, assessments can inform us of the potentialities God has built into us and of the qualities he has given to us as he has nurtured and guided us. But they are not always good predictors of the positions into which God wishes to place us. This is partly because there are other factors at stake than simply matching personality to position. Other factors may include the unavailability of someone more appropriate for the job. Ideally, we may not be the best person for a particular position, but we are, from God's or others' point of view, the best person for the moment. Or by casting us against type, God may wish to widen our own or other people's perceptions of what a position does or does not demand. Perhaps our efforts will galvanize someone to step up and do a more thorough job. Or it could be that God wants to display in and through us his divine versatility and power by enabling us to accomplish what under normal circumstances would be beyond our reach.

In addition, a person whose personality may not be seen as an ideal match for a position may bring a unique experience, perspective, and style to the task. At the very least, such a person may avoid falling too quickly into a business-as-usual approach. At the most, this person may need to rely on creative and experimental ways of tackling problems and may, by facing challenges, become an effective leader.

An analogy from cinema might be helpful here. In casting a film, a director usually chooses an actor whose persona and track record fit a particular role. In some cases, actors go through their entire career playing similar kinds of roles. Such roles, it is assumed, are what they do best. In the language of the trade, they are cast according to type. Occasionally, however, this rule of thumb is broken. The history of cinema contains some wonderful examples of actors who have managed to play a part at odds with their established persona. The results can be powerful. One thinks of such matinee idols as Cary Grant playing a Cockney crook in *None but the Lonely Heart,* Jean Simmons playing a manipulative and evil temptress in *Angel Face,* Tyrone Power playing a man who is seduced into the depths of depravity in *Nightmare Alley,* Robert Mitchum playing a timid schoolteacher in *Ryan's Daughter,* and Robin Williams playing a psychologically disturbed murderer in *Insomnia.* The struggle to play a role that differs from their usual persona often gives the performance an extra edge and strength.

Is Leadership Only about Fulfilling One's Potential or Relinquishing It to Fulfill Others'?

These days there is much talk about the importance of people fulfilling their potential. This involves actualizing and maximizing inherent gifts and learned capabilities and using them in the kinds of work for which one is best suited. There is, of course, something to all of this. People should be aware of their gifts and abilities, for they come from the Creator's hand or are the result of God's providence in their lives. Not acknowledging these things would be an act of ingratitude. The trouble with the language of fulfillment and potential is that it is too self-regarding and can too easily lead to self-centeredness. The focus is too resolutely on oneself and only secondarily on what one can do for others. If the words *fulfillment* and *potential* are used when discussing leadership, talk should focus on fulfilling others' potential. Paradoxically, as people seek to do that, genuine leadership takes place.

Power plays a role in the fulfillment of potential. Whether some people recognize it or not, making leadership a goal often springs from a latent desire to exercise power, to be in charge, to take control. As Max De Pree often says in workshops, even the most enlightened forms of leadership involve "meddling around in the lives of others." This is even more the case with less enlightened forms. Unless leaders exercise great care, they will have a tendency to coerce or manipulate those under their authority. This diminishes rather than fulfills their workers' potential and also hinders and distorts their own. The real task is to empower others, to play whatever part one can in enhancing their innate gifts and learned capacities so that they are able to contribute as fully and as creatively as possible to their organizations and to others.

Sometimes people realize that fulfilling their potential or even seeking to empower others springs too much from an unconscious or limited desire to focus on self rather than on others. This realization often takes place at the halfway stage in life when people reevaluate whether they have made the best use of their time.[9] Sometimes it occurs when they hit a personal or occupational wall. In such cases, people who are already in leadership positions may undergo a radical reevaluation of their life, leave behind much of what they have been doing, and take up a new form of work or way of working that is more other-focused. The story of one such person—who helped redefine power in more other-centered ways and contributed the idea of "hitting the wall" to workplace literature on spirituality—follows.

JANET HAGBERG: A FOR-PROFIT TO A NOT-FOR-PROFIT LEADER

Janet Hagberg was born in Minnesota to parents who seriously sought to live out evangelical Lutheran convictions. From a young age she attended church and several times underwent the experience of being born again. Through early efforts at playing the piano and singing in the choir, she became actively involved in the congregation. She also enjoyed and excelled at a private Christian high school that reinforced her church's strict, conservative pattern of belief and morality. Both her church and school emphasized sin and atonement at the expense of grace.

The dominant mood was one of guilt and shame, the dominant attitude one of unquestioning obedience. In this environment, she said, "I learned early to be a leader by getting involved and doing things . . . but at the same time, always wondering about all my myriads of questions."[10] In her late teens, she became a member of a crusade team that went to various parts of her state, providing opportunities for singing and speaking that both she and others regarded as a benchmark of genuine faith.

After completing high school, Hagberg attended the University of Minnesota. It was the 1960s, and the air was full of slogans such as "God is dead" and of protests against the Vietnam War. During this time, partly because of the more open atmosphere and partly because of a more academic approach to faith, she began to question the rigid, performance-oriented, literalist faith in which she had been raised. This resulted in a decade-long questioning of religious faith and practice, including a period of agnosticism. She became, by her own account, both intellectually factious and self-sufficient. Marriage after college to a pastor's son, who was also rebelling against the church, only exacerbated her questioning. She became an infrequent attender of a Unitarian church. The lack of a truly supportive community made it difficult for her to handle the additional spiritual issues that arose as a result of her mother's early death.

After completing her first degree, Hagberg began a master's program in psychology and social work, which became fields of alternative spiritual exploration. As she wrote later, "That led me into an adventure into humanistic psychology, creativity, psychic experiences, Eastern thought, meditation, other levels of consciousness, and New Age awareness. It was a whirlwind period of discovering new ways to be and think."[11] She gained a faculty position at the University of Minnesota, and everything she touched seemed to work out perfectly. Everything appeared to be going according to plan. She was unaware that her ability to realize her ambitions and her assumption that she had control over her life had heightened her vulnerability to the unexpected.

Riding this wave of achievement, she left the academic world to start her own business. She formed the Hagberg Company, a firm that specialized in training and management for business, higher education, and government. This too became highly successful. In time, she found herself called in to advise a range of Fortune 500 companies, among them Alcoa, Honeywell, and General Mills. Meanwhile, her involvement in adult education and government gave her the opportunity to try her hand at creating specialized programs. During the mid-1970s, in collaboration with a consultant involved in career development, she developed a program focusing on self and occupational renewal for the 3M Company. Its purpose was to help people explore new options and possibilities, both personally and vocationally, including life and career change. In 1978, this was released in book form and has since gone through several editions.[12] The book reveals a concern for being as well as doing, personal identity as well as career path, and leadership as well as vocational achievement. It stresses the need for both an inward and an outward journey, which is essential to a satisfactory and satisfying direction in life.

Ironically, it was around the time this program was published that her own life began to unravel. Her marriage fell apart, leading to divorce and a deep sense of personal failure. She began a period of self-examination during which she wrote in a journal, thought seriously about God, and began visiting churches—eventually finding one in Edina, Minnesota, that attracted other seekers and sought to help people keep head and heart, belief and life together. Through its loving and caring support, this community was instrumental in helping her regain her self-esteem and a renewed desire to achieve. She began to find a productive place in the church, using the skills she had employed so successfully in the business world, and it was not long before she began to take the lead in various projects both inside the church and in the wider community.

At the same time, her consulting work gained increasing attention, and she found herself reflecting more deeply on the nature, exercise, and abuse of power by individuals and institutions. Her book *Real Power,* she said, "was written for individuals who aspire to power, who long to understand what power really is; for leaders, to provoke their thinking about what true leadership is; for organizations, as a practical tool for developing people and vision for the future."[13] In this book, as noted earlier, Hagberg set out six stages or levels of power. In order they are powerlessness, power by association, power by symbols, power by reflection, and power by purpose. A final level, attained by very few, power by gestalt (or embodiment), is manifested chiefly as wisdom. This book, which developed out of not only Hagberg's substantial thinking about the issue but also her personal development and growth, was well received and is still considered by some to make the most sense of the various types of power at work in organizations. Its reception opened new doors for Hagberg's work as a consultant and led to further opportunities as a public speaker.

In all of this, Hagberg was responding to abilities she had and to opportunities that came her way but was also beginning to glimpse something deeper and more challenging. While she still had the desire to be a success and to conquer fresh fields, at a certain point, she became aware that despite her growing influence and recognition, something was still not quite right. She felt the need for a greater consistency between her work and her Christian faith. This led her to give up much of the consulting and training work she was doing to focus on understanding and becoming involved in spiritual direction. Increasingly, this became the focus of the time she spent with others in the workplace. Only by letting go of the reputation and status she had achieved was she able to enter into this.

Hagberg went on to cofound a nonprofit organization to eradicate the violence inflicted against women in spousal abuse. The organization is called Silent Witness, and their goal is zero cases of spousal abuse by 2010. Although Hagberg is the highest profile person in this organization, she deliberately takes a low-profile stance, encouraging, facilitating, and empowering others to undertake the work. As the organization grows in a grassroots way, she finds herself responding to its spontaneous growth rather than serving as a catalyst for it.

IMPLICATIONS

Enjoying the power and prestige that come with success is seductive because the more we receive, the more we want. Leaders who seek only to fulfill their own personal potential eventually fall prey to this seduction. But success for the sake of success is much like shaky scaffolding: Eventually, it becomes too weak to sustain the weight of power and prestige and falls to the ground.

Henri Nouwen offers an important insight into this question of self-fulfillment. Nouwen asks:

> What makes the temptation to power so seemingly irresistible? Maybe it is that power offers an easy substitute for the hard task of love. It seems easier to be God than to love God, easier to own life than to love life. . . . The temptation of power is greatest when intimacy is a threat.[14]

There are times when the desire to fulfill one's potential leads to emptiness, which is a lack of intimacy, and the yearning for something more. The longing to give one's life to work that goes beyond the immediacy of personal fulfillment—to contribute to something long-lasting—often occurs at the point in life when one is open to letting go of self-fulfillment in favor of service to others. At this juncture of letting go, a leader comes face-to-face with a critical and existential question: Am I doing the work to which I was called? Paul spoke of this in Philippians 3, where he makes a plea to continue pressing toward the goal and to "take hold of that for which Christ Jesus took hold of me" (Phil. 3:12). Paul rightly understood the importance of reaching for and firmly grasping one's calling. The challenge is to move from leadership built on power to leadership in which we critically discern where God is calling us to serve. For our work to be a calling, we must first know who we are and what we stand for. Sometimes it takes coming to grips with the emptiness of fulfilling one's own potential to discover these things.

Leadership is rooted in helping others fulfill their potential and letting go of one's need for self-fulfillment. As Robert Greenleaf so aptly put it, "The servant leader is servant first. It begins with the conscious feeling that one wants to serve first—and that conscious choice brings one to aspire to lead."[15] Janet Hagberg realized that her greatest contribution is to serve those who suffer spousal abuse and to take action to eradicate this form of violence. From this calling to serve came her aspiration to lead—to let go of self-fulfillment in favor of helping victims of abuse recover their potential.

Are Leaders Primarily Exercising Power or Empowering Others?

For most people, climbing the ladder of leadership is about attaining a position of power over resources, systems, and others. It is precisely this understanding of power, however, that has come under criticism in most of the recent literature on leadership. Max De Pree is fond of saying that, contrary to usual expectations, the more one climbs the corporate ladder, the more one becomes an amateur rather than an expert. The more responsibility a person has, the more that person has to know about everything. The more encompassing one's work, the more one realizes the multiple levels of complexity in an organization and the magnitude of decisions concerning it. Consequently, De Pree says, leaders need to know their limitations, become learners, and "abandon themselves to the strengths of others." Instead of regarding themselves as in control of an organization, good leaders know that control is in a range of hands, indeed, all the way down the line. They seek to recognize, affirm, and enhance the power of all involved. They view power as pervasive within or distributed throughout an organization. A leader's special responsibility is to discern where wisdom and expertise lie and then make the best use of both and help them develop further.

It is in empowering others that power is most effectively exercised and multiplied. Instead of this resulting in the diminution of a leader's power, it reveals its true nature and operation. As with self, according to Jesus in the Gospels, so with power: "Whoever loses his life . . . will save it" (Mark 8:35). For the most part, however, leaders find it in a different form. The more transformative forms of power will be most in evidence and are the most effective.

This discussion reveals yet another instance of a reversal of values that paradoxically results in things turning out for the best.

GORDON COSBY: A MISSION CHURCH LEADER

Gordon Cosby is not ranked among the high priests of church renewal in North America such as Bill Hybels, Chuck Swindoll, and Robert Schuller, or among the public figures engaged in creative mission such as Jim Wallis and Ray Bakke. Yet he has helped fashion one of the most innovative and influential congregations of the last half century whose members radically give their lives away to others in their immediate community as well as to people in the wider marketplace. Unlike most of his well-known peers, Cosby has hardly put anything into print, does not run a radio or a television ministry, and has not held seminars focusing on his church. He simply—and quietly—performs the job to which he feels called. He has no interest in creating disciples in his or his church's likeness. The church's name, Church of the Savior, is better known than his, and that is the way Cosby prefers it. He simply sees himself as facilitating the vision and mission of his church in the most committed, discerning, and empowering way.

Cosby is now in his mid-eighties. He was raised in a supportive and ecumenical family in Lynchburg, Virginia. He attended a Presbyterian church in the morning with one of his parents and a Baptist church in the evening with the other parent. In his mid-teens, he started to work among youth in the Baptist church and soon became close friends with the minister's daughter, Mary, whom he later married. In his early twenties, he attended simultaneously a college and a seminary. After he was ordained in 1942, he became a chaplain in the army and took part in the Normandy invasion. He was twice decorated for bravery under fire.

In the army, he concluded that the only way he could reach all the men in his regiment was to decentralize the work of the chapel by forming twelve fellowship and mission bands headed by the most spiritually mature men in each company. Each of these leaders had around him a committed core group. As a result of this experience, he began to dream of founding a church that would revolve around the quality of its members' commitment rather than the size of its membership and would also cut across denominational boundaries. This grew from his conviction that "no one had all the truth. Each of us had a part . . . and the best way to retain this truth . . . was to share it with others—to keep it by giving it away."[16] This was also true, he realized, of the way leadership operates: No one person, not even the designated leader of an organization, possesses the whole truth. It lies in the group and can be discovered only through everyone having a voice, listening carefully to others, and searching in the Spirit for a common mind.

After demobilization, Gordon and his wife began to frame a more concrete vision for such a community as well as look for a few others who might become founding members. After several months, a small group began to meet for corporate worship on Sunday afternoons in a borrowed church building, after which they would adjourn to a local restaurant for dinner. Conversation centered on how people's faith should impact their busy, weekday activities. Those who were interested attended weekly studies of the meaning of discipleship. Within two years, the church was able to purchase a four-story house in a run-down part of the city. It was refitted to include offices, a library, classrooms, a reception hall, a dining room, and a chapel. When the renovations were complete, a core group of nine people pledged to become a mission community that—to use Elton Trueblood's provocative words—took "unlimited liability" for one another over the long term. As the church's first brochure warned, doing this is "dangerous, for if one becomes committed in this way, all life will be different and every sphere of one's existence involved in the change."

In 1950, the church moved to a larger house. Even today the church has no identifiable church building. Its membership has grown but, by the standards of "successful" congregations, remains relatively small on account of the high level of commitment it requires. The church does not rely on one person; rather, each of its members learns how to pastor the others. Rather than being centralized in one place, the church has several congregations, each of which is also a mission. They meet at a coffeehouse, a housing project, an arts center, a renewal farm, and a suburban home. All are organized and led by their members. This way of being the church and doing mission runs counter to traditional Christian culture.

From the outset, all major decisions were made by the entire community. While, in the initial stages, Cosby often exhibited more discernment than others as to the way forward, this was not always the case. He and his wife expected and encouraged others to be involved in strategic planning, and frequently a specific vision or plan of action emerged from someone else in the group or as a result of group reflection. In such cases, Cosby energetically supported whatever decisions were made and whoever was chosen to implement them. As the church grew, other congregations were formed. The size of these groups allowed the members to maintain the quality of relationships and accountability experienced by the original group and also distributed the pastoral care of members throughout the entire congregation. Another empowering structure was a class in which each member received help from the others to discern his or her calling. From the earliest days, there was never a sense that their service was primarily an extension of their pastor's work.

As for Cosby himself, he was bound by the same covenant, shared equally in the life of the community, and like everyone else was accountable to its members. He did not operate from a privileged position in the congregation but as one among them. Though he could and often did speak prophetically, his views had power primarily because of the credibility he had gained through his daily and down-to-earth participation in the community. Like everyone else, he was also involved in serving and rebuilding the local neighborhood. Rather than diminishing Cosby's influence in the church, however, his actions and equal status supported the church's ethos and way of operating.

The most important development in the church's life and, in some respects, the most vital test and demonstration of Cosby's approach to leadership took place in the 1970s. Membership in the church had grown to over one hundred members. Cosby declared that he could no longer fulfill his general pastoral responsibility in the community. He could not give sufficient support even to those who were most active in the congregation and in mission. He suggested that they could either add more church staff or decentralize the operation by dividing the church into smaller units and giving more authority to others.

"Is it possible," he asked, "that we can divide into different combinations cohering around different worship centers and, in the process of creating the new, not losing what we value? There are many, many people in the life of this community with rare gifts of leadership that are not being used. . . . It can be exciting, if we do not decide to hang on . . . [but] trust that the same Spirit which brought us to this point will still be around. We as an organization have been blessed, and my guess is that leadership might be developed at an even deeper level than we have known it."[17] This challenge was the beginning of a wholesale restructuring of the church into a cluster of mission congregations, each with its own leadership and decision-making processes. Although Cosby remained part of the core group to which each center was accountable, he was in no sense the key figure and influence in the various centers.

Although, from one point of view, Cosby increasingly divested himself of leadership in the congregation, from another he demonstrated how profound his practice of it was. He refused to be the one to whom others always looked for guidance and instead released them to take the lead and then assisted in any way he could. What was at the heart of Cosby's capacity to do this? According to Elizabeth O'Connor, a key member of the community and the chief chronicler of its activities, it is his "willingness to question" and his readiness "to give up the old and embrace the new."[18] This springs, she says, from a wonderful "flexibility of spirit." Cosby also displays an acute capacity to listen to God, not only in moments of withdrawal but also in the most ordinary situations. For example, the idea for a coffeehouse that would be a hospitable place not only for church members but also for people in the neighborhood looking for a place to hang out did not come during a time of secluded prayer but as Cosby reflected on the liveliness and interaction in a tavern compared to a dull church service he had just visited. "I realized that there was more warmth and fellowship in that tavern than there was in the church. If Jesus of Nazareth had his choice He would probably have come to the tavern rather than to the church we visited."[19]

Cosby also has a commitment to affirm others. Because he "gives to those he touches a sense of worth and destiny," it is not surprising that others gravitate toward him and feel empowered by him. His belief that everyone can be a special person of God means that ordinary members of the church are "entrusted in ways it has not seen before."[20] Because he is committed to helping people become who God wants them to be and doing what God wants them to do, he can give freedom to each of the mission communities to find and implement its own vision.

IMPLICATIONS

Some years ago, a theological student attended a cluster of informal churches meeting in homes to learn more about a nontraditional way of being and doing church. The first meeting he attended began mid-morning and ran over lunch until early afternoon. There were roughly twenty-five people present. Every so often during the gathering, he wrote down something that struck or puzzled him. When the meeting ended, he went over to a small group of people and thanked them for their hospitality in allowing him to observe. "There is, however, one aspect of your time together that particularly puzzles me," he said.

"And what's that?" asked one of the others. "Well, although I kept a careful watch of what took place, I was not able to determine who your leader is!" So many people had participated in such a variety of ways that no one person had stood out from the rest. As it happened, one couple had played a major role in providing a framework for the service, but they had not been visible during the service.

This is often the case when a commitment to empowering others rather than exercising power over others is at work. Much empowering takes place out of the spotlight. While it may seem easier for this to happen at the kind of meeting just described, it can also occur at larger, more public occasions. For example, a three-day national consultation was discreetly facilitated by Leighton Ford. Anyone present would have found it extremely difficult to identify him as the key instigator and leader of the event. Likewise, anyone walking into the coffee shop known as the Potter's House in downtown Washington would find it difficult to pinpoint the key person in the network of congregations and missions of which it is a part. In the broad cross section of people, one would be hard-pressed to pick the elderly man engaged in a relaxed conversation at one of the tables.

Conclusion: The Future of Leadership

Not long ago, Max De Pree asked a paradoxical question: Does leadership have a future?[21] Intertwined in this provocative question is concern about the rising ineffectiveness and selfishness among leaders. If leadership is to have a future, some important principles need to be preserved. These principles can be illuminated by asking the right questions. While good leaders do not have all the answers, they should possess the wisdom and the insight to raise important questions that search for deeper meaning. Such questions are critical because they help leaders and organizations find and determine their direction. The leaders just profiled asked some powerful questions of themselves and those around them. Some of their questions correspond with those De Pree sees as important. If leadership is to have a future, these questions must be addressed.

Who do I intend to be? This is not the same as asking, "What do I intend to do?" which is always a consequence of who one intends to be. A person can find out the latter by asking, "What do I believe? What is my purpose in life? To what am I, as a leader, devoted?" These raise the issues of purpose, virtue, and truth, all of which lead to hope. Without purpose, virtue, and truth, it is difficult to experience hope. An absence of virtues and the presence of deceit do not create the conditions necessary for hope to survive. For leadership to endure, it must be intertwined with hope—hope in the sense of looking forward to the future with expectation. If leadership has a future, leaders must be able to articulate, find, and live out their own sense of hope. Hope grows dim as people deviate from their core values and grows stronger and becomes contagious in the context of shared hope within a community.

What is the source of our humanity? As Christians, we believe that the source of our humanity is found in being created in God's image. This has profound implications for how to treat people in organizations. Seeing each person as created in God's image compels leaders to offer respect, create opportunities for contribution, and affirm the gifts of others.

In the company cafeteria, how good should the bagels be? This is a question of quality. Society seems to care more about numbers than quality, particularly in an increasingly competitive marketplace. What is the quality of our relationships, and what do things such as opportunity, access, and reconciliation have to do with quality?

What will I die for? In other words, what is most essential, what matters most? This is a question of purpose and integrity. When leaders have a clear sense of calling, they serve as models and mentors for others to find and live out their callings.

What may a leader not delegate? For leadership to thrive, leaders need to be clear about what they alone can and therefore must do. Leaders build and maintain trust as well as share responsibilities. They hold both themselves and the organizations they serve accountable. One thing they do not delegate is the obligation to be prepared to lead.[22]

Lastly, De Pree points to four critical questions that leaders must ponder consistently over the course of their leading:

1. What is my purpose in life?
2. What do I owe?
3. What will I promise?
4. What may I keep?

De Pree insightfully notes that as a society we need to care more about faithfulness than success, more about the potential of communities than individual accomplishment, and more about inclusiveness than winning. The values of society are not always the best guide and indeed often fail to reflect the true essence of leadership. If leadership is to survive, there must be an environment of high moral standards among leaders and followers, and this has the best chance of coming to expression as faith-based leaders live out their core convictions and Christian faith in everyday life and work.

The second factor that is critical for the future of leadership is the finding or creating of conducive contexts in which leadership can most effectively develop. Leadership does not come merely from gaining knowledge about it through a set of seminars or a course, though these may certainly be helpful. Some of what is entailed in faithful leadership can come through observing those who embody and practice it. But more is needed.

First of all, leaders must place people in self-directed teams with intrinsic as well as extrinsic rewards for their performance. People can learn from those working with them how to identify, handle, and evaluate issues related to faithfulness. Group wisdom has much to offer, even when people tackle issues in different ways. Where possible, tackling situations in pairs rather than alone can increase learning curves and improve responses. When there is no agreement on the best course of action, observing the ways others deal with issues allows people to see the strengths and weaknesses of different approaches.

Second, people should be encouraged to become involved in a voluntary organization. In such a setting, acceptance and influence are earned differently, for example, by showing a commitment to the purpose of the organization and by exhibiting a capacity to work well with others. Leighton Ford has said that anyone seeking to become a leader in the church should first gain some experience in the voluntary sector. This is the best context in which to learn whether one has the qualities and attributes required for leadership in a changing world and among the coming generation. Only earned not expected authority will now do. In the same way, direct participation in nonprofit organizations creates opportunities for leaders to use and improve their skills. For example, it can help them move from a reward mentality to a service mind-set, or from a rugged individualism to a commitment to the general good.

Third, people should be shown the benefit of being part of an informal group of people at a similar level. When trust is present in such a group, people feel free to discuss questions related to faithfulness and to ask for help with individual struggles in this area.

In addition, there is always a place for ongoing connections with people who already exhibit faithful leading at work. Much can be gained from a mentoring experience. Anyone who invites a mentoree into such a relationship or finds a mentor with whom he or she can meet several times a year is bound to enhance the prospects for the future of leadership.

conclusion

Max De Pree, the acclaimed author and former chairman of the board and CEO of Herman Miller, Inc. and to whom this book is dedicated, knows a great deal about creating a legacy. During his stint as CEO from 1980 to 1987, profits at the office furniture manufacturer soared, and people in the company excelled. His values-based leadership earned him a spot in *Fortune* magazine's National Business Hall of Fame, and the Business Enterprise Trust awarded him the Lifetime Achievement Award for his innovative approach to business.

Max's father, D. J. De Pree, founded Herman Miller in the 1920s, grew it, and handed it over to his oldest son, Hugh, in 1962. When Hugh retired in 1980, he passed the torch to Max, who was a vice president in the company at the time. Max understood well the legacy he had inherited from his father and his brother, and he continued to build on the spirit and the practices established by his predecessors. In the following excapt from his third book, *Leading without Power: Finding Hope in Serving Community,* he reflects on the idea of legacy:

> It's important to distinguish between strategic planning and leaving a legacy. A strategic plan is a long-term commitment to something we intend to do. A legacy results from the facts of our behavior that remain in the minds of others, the cumulative, informal record of how close we came to the person we intended to be. It is important to remember that what we do will always be a consequence of who we become. What you plan to do differs enormously from what you leave behind. Becoming an effective leader requires us to think purposefully about legacy. Everyone leaves a legacy, a legacy may consist of words, a building, a single deed. One powerful moment may be our legacy, and we may not even realize it at the time. We must think consciously about what kind of legacy we want to leave our organizations, our communities, and our families.[1]

According to De Pree, building a legacy is intentional and takes place over time through actions. It involves the following dimensions:

- *Establishing and maintaining good relationships.* This is at the center of organizational life. Effective leaders cannot be successful without mastering relationships. Relational competence derives from selflessness and real concern for people and is based on understanding and acting on the truth that people are created in the image of God. Competence in relationships results in civility, love, and devotion to a common good. Nothing guarantees it; no leader succeeds without it.

- *Formulating a direction that is clearly observable.* A legacy always reflects a vision. A clear sense of direction is the necessary foundation for a life of service.

- *Defending the truth.* Truth has to be the first level of quality. Without truth, people react in a temporary way to daily pressures. A legacy helps others preserve and illuminate the truth. Truth can become part of a legacy only when it is lived.

- *Becoming personally accountable.* Many circumstances in life cannot be controlled, but a person can make the choice to accept responsibility for himself or herself and not to deprive others of this important aspect of life.

- *Setting standards that endure.* Such standards are not just of performance but also of dignity and servanthood, good manners, good taste, and decorum. Society cries out for the civility that results from high standards.

- *Lifting the spirits of others.* A spirit-lifting presence is an important part of a legacy. Leaders who have the gift to lift the spirits of those with whom they work inspire others to do the same.

- *Developing constructive constraints and simplicity in work.* Constraints for creative people are not a problem but an opportunity and a guide. Ability does not mandate use. The most powerful people wield their power carefully.

- *Striving to integrate life and faith.* This involves bringing work up to the standards of beliefs and acting on those beliefs.

- *Enabling others to live up to their full potential.* A legacy extends beyond a person and enables others to achieve. Mentoring, which can happen unintentionally, is a way to pass on wisdom, knowledge, and experience.

- *Saying thank you to the organization and the people with whom one works.* Work can become an expression of gratitude for the chance to contribute. What a person leaves behind, more than anything that person does or says, tells the world what he or she thought of the organization and its work.[2]

A leadership legacy is something that is built over time during each day of one's life. Are we ready for the moment when our convictions will be tested? Have we taken the long view and considered what our actions today will mean years from now? When we think in terms of legacy, work and life take on a new meaning and purpose, and we see things from a new perspective. It is then that our leadership is fully realized, and, if God grants it, it will continue to exercise its influence long after we have passed from the scene.

notes

Chapter 1

1. Peter G. Northouse, *Leadership: Theory and Practice* (Thousand Oaks, Calif.: Sage, 2001).

2. Abraham Zaleznik, "Managers and Leaders: Are They Different?" *Harvard Business Review on Leadership* (Cambridge: Harvard Business School Press, 1998), 67–70.

3. James Clawson, *Level Three Leadership: Getting below the Surface,* 2d ed. (Upper Saddle River, N.J.: Prentice-Hall, 1999).

4. Henry Mintzberg, "The Manager's Job: Folklore and Fact," *Harvard Business Review on Leadership* (Cambridge: Harvard Business School Press, 1998), 24.

5. See Zaleznik, "Managers and Leaders," 76.

6. Ibid., 87.

7. See T. W. Adorno, E. Frenkel-Brunswick, D. J. Levinson, and N. Sanford, *The Authoritarian Personality* (New York: Wiley & Sons, 1964).

8. Linda Hill and Suzi Wetlaufer, "Leadership When There Is No One to Ask: An Interview with ENI's Franco Bernabe," *Harvard Business Review* (July–August 1988): 81–94.

9. Warren Bennis, *Why Leaders Can't Lead: The Unconscious Conspiracy Continues* (San Francisco: Jossey-Bass, 1989).

10. Wilfred H. Drath and Charles J. Palus, *Making Common Sense: Leadership as Meaning-Making in a Community of Practice* (Greensboro, N.C.: Center for Creative Leadership, 1994).

11. Ronald A. Heifetz, *Leadership without Easy Answers* (Cambridge: Belknap Press of Harvard University Press, 1994); cf. John M. Bryson and Barbara C. Crosby, *Leadership for the Common Good: Tackling Public Problems in a Shared-Power World* (San Francisco: Jossey-Bass, 1992).

12. Garry Wills, *Certain Trumpets: The Call of Leaders* (New York: Simon & Schuster, 1994).

13. Bill Hybels, "Finding Your Leadership Style: Ten Different Ways to Lead God's People," *Leadership* (winter 1998): 84–89.

14. Tom Peters, "Rule #3: Leadership Is as Confusing as Hell," *Fast Company* 44 (March 2001): 124–40.

15. Gareth Morgan, *Images of Organization* (London: Sage, 1986), 11–17. For a typology of historic approaches to change, see the appendix to Dexter Dunphy and Andrew Griffiths,

137

The Sustainable Corporation: Organisational Renewal in Australia (Sydney: Allen & Unwin, 1999), 205–9.

16. See John S. Evans, *The Management of Human Capacity: An Approach to the Ideas of Elliott Jacques* (Bradford, Eng.: MCB Human Resources, 1979).

17. John Naisbitt and Patricia Aburdene, *Megatrends 2000: Ten New Directions for the 1990s* (New York: Morrow, 1990), 36.

18. U.S. Department of Labor Statistics, 1998, *Employment and Earnings* 45, no. 1 (1998): 163.

19. Fortune 1000 List, *Fortune,* 13 October 2003, 105–8.

20. Deborah Swiss, *Women Breaking Through: Overcoming the Final Ten Obstacles at Work* (Princeton, N.J.: Peterson's/Pacesetter Books, 1996), 1.

21. Ibid., 7–10.

22. Jennifer James, *Thinking in the Future Tense: Leadership Skills for a New Age* (New York: Simon & Schuster, 1996), 214.

23. Ibid., 218.

24. Ibid., 226.

25. Laura L. Nash, *Believers in Business* (Nashville: Thomas Nelson, 1994), 37.

26. Walter Brueggemann, Sharon Parks, and Thomas H. Groome, *To Act Justly, Love Tenderly, Walk Humbly: An Agenda for Ministers* (New York: Paulist Press, 1986).

27. Janet O. Hagberg, *Real Power: Stages of Personal Power in Organizations* (Salem, Wis.: Sheffield, 1994), xxi.

28. Ibid.

Chapter 2

1. See Robert Banks, *Paul's Idea of Community: The Early House Churches in Their Historical Setting* (Peabody, Mass.: Hendrickson, 1994); and idem, "Pauline Church Order and Governance," in *Dictionary of Paul and His Letters,* ed. Gerald F. Hawthorne and Ralph P. Martin (Downers Grove, Ill.: InterVarsity, 1993), 131–37; as well as Helen Doohan, *Leadership in Paul* (Wilmington, Del.: Michael Glazier, 1984); J. Oswald Sanders, *Paul the Leader: A Vision for Christian Leadership Today* (Eastbourne, Eng.: Kingsway, 1983); and Stacy T. Rinehart, *Upside Down: The Paradox of Servant Leadership* (Colorado Springs: NavPress, 1998), 94–98, 106–7.

2. See Banks, "Pauline Church Order and Governance," 131–37.

3. Sanders, *Paul the Leader,* 69–111.

4. See Mark O'Keefe, O.S.B, "The Benedictine Abbot: Creative Tensions in Leadership" (unpublished paper for the De Pree Leadership Center, Pasadena, Calif., 1999).

5. Timothy F. Lull, "Underachievers? Or Reformers? Lutherans Exercising Daily Life Leadership" (paper presented at the meeting Traditions in Leadership, De Pree Leadership Center, Pasadena, Calif., June 1999).

6. See Herman Bavinck, *Our Reasonable Faith: A Survey of Christian Doctrine* (Grand Rapids: Eerdmans, 1956), 32.

7. Richard J. Mouw, "Leadership and the Threefold Office of Christ" (paper presented at the meeting Traditions in Leadership, De Pree Leadership Center, Pasadena, Calif., June 1999).

8. Elizabeth B. Keiser and R. Melvin Keiser, "Quaker Principles in the Crucible of Practice," *Cross Currents* 43, no. 4 (winter 1993): 476–84.

9. Robert Lawrence Smith, *A Quaker Book of Wisdom: Life Lessons in Simplicity, Service, and Common Sense* (New York: Eagle Brook, 1998), 182.

10. Richard J. Wood, "Christ Has Come to Teach His People Himself: Quaker Ambiguities about Leadership" (paper presented at the meeting Traditions in Leadership, De Pree Leadership Center, Pasadena, Calif., June 1999).

11. Cecil M. Robeck, "A Pentecostal Perspective on Leadership" (paper presented at the meeting Traditions in Leadership, De Pree Leadership Center, Pasadena, Calif., June 1999).

12. See, for example, G. P. Gooch, *English Democratic Ideas in the Seventeenth Century* (New York: Harper, 1959).

13. James MacGregor Burns, *Leadership* (New York: Harper & Row, 1978).

14. Ralph M. Stogdill, "Personal Factors Associated with Leadership," *Journal of Psychology* 25 (1948): 35–71.

15. Ralph M. Stogdill, *Handbook of Leadership: A Survey of Theory and Research* (New York: Free Press, 1974).

16. The latest version is Robert R. Blake and Jane S. Mouton, *The Managerial Grid III: A New Look at the Classic That Has Boosted Productivity and Profits for Thousands of Corporations Worldwide* (Houston: Gulf, 1985).

17. Gary A. Yukl, *Leadership in Organizations* (Englewood Cliffs, N.J.: Prentice-Hall, 1989).

18. Fred E. Fiedler, *A Theory of Leadership Effectiveness* (New York: McGraw-Hill, 1967).

19. Paul Hersey, Kenneth H. Blanchard, and Dewey E. Johnson, *Management of Organizational Behavior: Utilizing Human Resources* (Upper Saddle River, N.J.: Prentice-Hall, 1996).

20. James MacGregor Burns, *Leadership* (New York: Harper & Row, 1978).

21. Alan Bryman, *Charisma and Leadership in Organizations* (London: Sage, 1992).

22. Bernard M. Bass, *Leadership and Performance beyond Expectations* (New York: Free Press, 1985); and idem, *Transformational Leadership: Industrial, Military, and Educational Impact* (Mahwah, N.J.: Lawrence Earlbaum, 1998).

23. Warren Bennis and Burt Nanus, *Leaders: Strategies for Taking Charge*, rev. ed. (New York: Harper & Row, 1997).

24. See further Warren Bennis, *On Becoming a Leader* (Reading, Mass.: Perseus Books, 1994), 39–42; and Burt Nanus, *The Leader's Edge: The Seven Keys to Leadership in a Turbulent World* (Chicago: Contemporary Books, 1989), 81–97.

25. Allan R. Cohen and David L. Bradford, *Influence without Authority* (New York: Wiley, 1990).

26. Wilfred H. Drath and Charles J. Palus, *Making Common Sense: Leadership as Meaning-Making in a Community of Practice* (Greensboro, N.C.: Center for Creative Leadership, 1994).

27. Laura L. Nash, *Believers in Business* (Nashville: Thomas Nelson, 1994).

28. Denise Shekerjian, *Uncommon Genius: How Great Ideas Are Born* (New York: Penguin, 1990), 101–2.

Chapter 3

1. Stephen Pattison, *The Faith of the Managers: When Management Becomes Religion* (London: Cassell, 1997).

2. Stephen Pattison, "Recognizing Leaders' Hidden Beliefs," in *Faith and Leadership: How Leaders Live Out Their Faith in Their Work and Why It Matters,* ed. Robert Banks and Kim Powell (San Francisco: Jossey-Bass, 2000), 169–81.

3. Ibid., 171.

4. Ibid., 179–80.

5. Stephen R. Covey, *The Seven Habits of Highly Effective People: Restoring the Character Ethic* (New York: Simon & Schuster, 1989).

6. Stephen R. Covey, *Principle-Centered Leadership* (New York: Summit Books, 1991).

7. Stephen R. Covey, A. Roger Merrill, and Rebecca R. Merrill, *First Things First: To Live, to Love, to Learn, to Leave a Legacy* (New York: Simon & Schuster, 1994).

8. Alan Wolfe, "White Magic: Capitalism, Mormonism, and the Doctrines of Stephen Covey," *The New Republic,* 23 February 1998, 26–34.

9. Covey, *Principle-Centered Leadership,* 40–47.

10. Ibid., 33–39.

11. Wolfe, "White Magic," 32.

12. As in Jay A. Conger, ed., *Spirit at Work: Discovering the Spirituality in Leadership* (San Francisco: Jossey-Bass, 1994).

13. Cf. James Hillman, *The Soul's Code: In Search of Character and Calling* (New York: Random House, 1996); Jack Hawley, *Reawakening the Spirit in Work: The Power of Dharmic Management* (San Francisco: Berrett-Koehler, 1993); and Alan Briskin, *The Stirring of Soul in the Workplace* (San Francisco: Jossey-Bass, 1996).

14. Cf. William C. Miller, "How Do We Put Our Spiritual Values to Work?" in *New Traditions in Business: Spirit and Leadership in the Twenty-First Century,* ed. John Renesch (San Francisco: Berrett-Koehler, 1992), 69–77; Matthew Fox, *The Reinvention of Work: A New Vision of Livelihood for Our Time* (San Francisco: HarperSanFrancisco, 1994); Gay Hendricks and Kate Ludeman, *The Corporate Mystic: A Guidebook for Visionaries with Their Feet on the Ground* (New York: Bantam Books, 1996); Carol Orsborn, *Inner Excellence: Spiritual Principles of Life-Driven Business* (San Rafael, Calif.: New World Library, 1992); and the interviews with Matthew Fox, Keshavan Nair, and Barry Schieber in Charles Garfield, with Michael Toms, *The Soul of Business: New Dimensions* (Carlsbad, Calif.: Hay House, 1997), 73–98, 123–46, 169–92.

15. Lee G. Bolman and Terrence E. Deal, *Leading with Soul: An Uncommon Journey of Spirit* (San Francisco: Jossey-Bass, 1995).

16. Russ S. Moxley, *Leadership and Spirit: Breathing New Vitality and Energy into Individuals and Organizations* (San Francisco: Jossey-Bass, 2000).

17. Ibid., xiv.

18. Ibid., 24.

19. Peter B. Vaill, *Spirited Leading and Learning: Process Wisdom for a New Age* (San Francisco: Jossey-Bass, 1998).

20. Charles Hartshorne, *Reality as Social Process: Studies in Metaphysics and Religion* (Glencoe, Ill.: Free Press, 1953).

21. Vaill, *Spirited Leading,* 5.

22. Ibid., 179.

23. Ibid., 180.

24. Ibid., 208.

25. Ibid., 219.

26. Ibid., 208.

27. James W. Sire, *Václav Havel: The Intellectual Conscience of International Politics: An Introduction, Appreciation, and Critique* (Downers Grove, Ill.: InterVarsity, 2001).

28. John C. Haughey, "A Leader's Conscience: The Integrity and Spirituality of Václav Havel," in *Spirit at Work*, 43.

29. Václav Havel, *Disturbing the Peace: A Conversation with Karel Hvizdala*, trans. Paul Wilson (New York: Knopf, 1990), 199.

30. Ibid., 120, 123.

31. Václav Havel, *Letters to Olga: June 1979–September 1982*, trans. Paul Wilson (New York: Holt, 1989), 331–33.

32. Sire, *Václav Havel*, 98.

33. Havel, *Disturbing the Peace*, 102.

34. J. Vladilav, ed., *Václav Havel, or Living in Truth* (London: Faber & Faber, 1986), 12.

35. Havel, *Disturbing the Peace*, 8.

36. Václav Havel, "The Revolution Has Just Begun," *Time*, 5 March 1990, 14–15.

37. Havel, *Disturbing the Peace*, 203.

38. Ibid., 204–5.

39. Cf. John C. Haughey, *Converting 9 to 5: A Spirituality of Daily Work* (New York: Crossroad, 1989); Parker J. Palmer, *The Active Life: A Spirituality of Work, Creativity, and Caring* (San Francisco: Harper & Row, 1990); William E. Diehl, *The Monday Connection: A Spirituality of Competence, Affirmation, and Support in the Workplace* (San Francisco: HarperSanFrancisco, 1991); Steve Jacobsen, *Hearts to God, Hands to Work: Connecting Spirituality and Work* (Washington, D.C.: Alban Institute, 1997); and most recently, Gregory F. A. Pierce, *Spirituality at Work: Ten Ways to Balance Your Life on the Job* (Chicago: Loyola, 2001).

40. Patricia D. Brown, *Learning to Lead from Your Spiritual Center* (Nashville: Abingdon, 1996).

41. Ibid., 11.

42. Ibid.

43. Max De Pree, *Leading without Power: Finding Hope in Serving Community* (San Francisco: Jossey-Bass, 1997).

Chapter 4

1. Keshavan Nair, *A Higher Standard of Leadership: Lessons from the Life of Gandhi* (San Francisco: Berrett-Koehler, 1994); Joel Edelman and Mary Beth Crain, *The Tao of Negotiation: How You Can Prevent, Resolve, and Transcend Conflict in Work and Everyday Life* (New York: HarperBusiness, 1993); James A. Autry and Stephen Mitchell, *Real Power: Business Lessons from the Tao Te Ching* (New York: Riverhead Books, 1999); John Renesch, *Leadership in a New Era: Visionary Perspectives on the Big Issues of Our Time* (San Francisco: New Leaders Press, 1994); some of the essays in John Renesch, ed., *New Traditions in Business: Spirit and Leadership in the Twenty-First Century* (San Francisco: Berrett-Koehler, 1992); and Lee G. Bolman and Terrence E. Deal, *Leading with Soul: An Uncommon Journey of Spirit* (San Francisco: Jossey-Bass, 1995). Others have drawn on the New Science, often drawing out its spiritual implications. Such works include Joseph Jaworski, *Synchronicity: The Inner Path of Leadership* (San Francisco: Berrett-Koehler, 1996); and Margaret J. Wheatley, *Leadership and the New Science: Learning about Organization from an Orderly Universe* (San Francisco: Berrett-Koehler, 1992).

2. James Autry, *Confessions of an Accidental Businessman* (San Francisco: Berrett-Koehler, 1996); John Beckett, *Loving Monday* (Downers Grove, Ill.: InterVarsity, 1998); Kenneth Blanchard, Bill Hybels, and Phil Hodges, *Leadership by the Book: Tools to Transform Your Workplace* (New York: Morrow, 1999); Tom Chappell, *The Soul of a Business: Managing for Profit and the Common Good* (New York: Bantam Books, 1993); Ken Melrose, *Making the Grass Greener on Your Side: A CEO's Journey to Leading by Serving* (San Francisco: Berrett-Koehler, 1995); Michael Novak, *Business as a Calling: Work and the Examined Life* (New York: Free Press, 1996); C. William Pollard, *The Soul of the Firm* (New York: HarperBusiness, 1996); some material in Jay Conger, ed., *Spirit at Work: Discovering the Spirituality in Leadership* (San Francisco: Jossey-Bass, 1994); and Larry C. Spears, ed., *Insights on Leadership: Service, Stewardship, Spirit, and Servant-Leadership* (New York: Wiley, 1998), 197–267. Two substantial empirically based studies of the way religiously inclined leaders function are Laura L. Nash, *Believers in Business* (Nashville: Thomas Nelson, 1994); and Perry Pascarella, *Christ-Centered Leadership: Thriving in Business by Putting God in Charge* (Rocklin, Calif.: Prima, 1999).

3. David Baron and Lynette Padwa, *Moses on Management: Fifty Leadership Lessons from the Greatest Manager of All Time* (New York: Pocket Books, 1999).

4. Ibid., 278–84.

5. In the preface to Laura Beth Jones, *Jesus CEO: Using Ancient Wisdom for Visionary Leadership* (New York: Hyperion, 1995). Other books along similar lines are Bob Briner, *The Leadership Lessons of Jesus: A Timeless Model for Today's Leaders* (Nashville: Broadman & Holman, 1997); and Bob Briner and Ray Pritchard, *More Leadership Lessons of Jesus: A Timeless Model for Today's Leaders* (Nashville: Broadman & Holman, 1998).

6. Ibid., 295–302.

7. Ibid., 296–99.

8. Ibid., 16.

9. Ibid., 17.

10. Ibid., 295.

11. Charles C. Manz, *The Leadership Wisdom of Jesus: Practical Lessons for Today* (San Francisco: Berrett-Koehler, 1998).

12. Max De Pree, *Leadership Is an Art* (New York: Doubleday, 1989); idem, *Leadership Jazz* (New York: Doubleday Currency, 1992); and idem, *Leading without Power: Finding Hope in Serving Community* (San Francisco: Jossey-Bass, 1997).

13. Jeffrey L. Cruikshank and Clark Malcolm, *Herman Miller, Inc.: Buildings and Beliefs* (Washington, D.C.: American Institute of Architects Press, 1994).

14. De Pree, *Leading without Power,* 127–29.

15. Ibid.

16. Andrew T. Le Peau, *Paths of Leadership: Guiding Others toward Growth in Christ through Serving, Following, Teaching, Modeling, Envisioning* (Downers Grove, Ill.: InterVarsity, 1983).

17. Leighton Ford, *Jesus: The Transforming Leader* (London: Hodder & Stoughton, 1991).

18. See Robert Banks, *Reenvisioning Theological Education: Exploring a Missional Alternative to Current Models* (Grand Rapids: Eerdmans, 1999).

19. Henry Cadbury, *The Peril of Modernizing Jesus* (London: SPCK, 1962), 4.

20. Ibid., 9.

21. Bruce Barton, *The Man Nobody Knows* (Indianapolis: Bobbs Merrill, 1925), 11.

22. Ibid., 123–24.

23. Ibid., 141–42.

24. Ibid., 77.

25. Ibid., 99–100.

26. Ibid., 101–2.

27. See Stanley Hauerwas, "Jesus: The Presence of the Kingdom," in *The Peaceable Kingdom: A Primer in Christian Ethics* (Philadelphia: SCM, 1983), 72–95.

28. Ibid., 96–115.

29. Christian Schumacher, *To Live and Work: A Theological Interpretation* (Bromley, Eng.: Marc, 1987); and idem, *God in Work: Discovering the Divine Pattern for Work in the New Millennium* (Oxford, Eng.: Lion Publishing, 1998).

30. Dorothy L. Sayers, *The Mind of the Maker* (London: Methuen, 1941).

31. Gordon Preece, *A Trinitarian Perspective on Work* (New York: Edward Mellen, 1998).

32. Jurgen Moltmann, *The Trinity and the Kingdom of God* (Philadelphia: Fortress, 1993); and Miroslav Volf, *Work in the Spirit: Toward a Theology of Work* (New York: Oxford, 1991).

33. Catherine Mowry LaCugna, *God for Us: The Trinity and Christian Life* (San Francisco: HarperCollins, 1993).

34. Peter M. Senge, *The Fifth Discipline: The Art and Practice of the Learning Organization* (New York: Doubleday Currency, 1990).

35. Russ S. Moxley, *Leadership and Spirit: Breathing New Vitality and Energy into Individuals and Organizations* (San Francisco: Jossey-Bass, 2000).

36. Max De Pree, "What Is Leadership?" in *Leading Organizations: Perspectives for a New Era,* ed. Gill Robinson Hickman (Thousand Oaks, Calif.: Sage, 1998), 131.

37. Peter Block and Peter Koestenbaum, *Freedom and Accountability at Work: Applying Philosophical Insight to the Real World* (San Francisco: Jossey-Bass, 2001), 30.

38. Stacy T. Rinehart, *Upside Down: The Paradox of Servant Leadership* (Colorado Springs: NavPress, 1998).

39. Ibid., 88–90, 104–6. For a critique of the Orthodox view of the Trinity as too hierarchical and containing no democratic element, see Miroslav Volf, *Trinity and Community: An Ecumenical Ecclesiology* (Grand Rapids: Eerdmans, 1997), where the writings of John D. Zizioulas, especially his *Being as Communion: Studies in Personhood and the Church* (Crestwood, N.Y.: St. Vladimir's Seminary Press, 1985), are particularly in view.

40. Benjamin D. Williams and Michael T. McKibben, *Oriented Leadership: Why All Christians Need It* (Wayne, N.J.: Orthodox Christian Publications Center, 1994).

41. Ibid., 22–23.

42. Ibid., 24, 29.

43. Ibid., 139.

44. John Goldingay, *Men Behaving Badly* (Exeter, Eng.: Paternoster, 2000).

45. Walter C. Wright, *Relational Leadership: A Biblical Model for Leadership Service* (Exeter, Eng.: Paternoster, 2000).

46. J. Robert Clinton, *The Making of a Leader: Recognizing the Lessons and Stages of Leadership Development* (Colorado Springs: NavPress, 1988).

47. Ibid., 181.

48. J. Robert Clinton, "The Emerging Leader," *Theology, News, and Notes* (June 1987): 28.

49. Robert Banks, ed., *Faith Goes to Work: Reflections from the Marketplace* (Washington, D.C.: Alban Institute, 1993), 18–30.

50. William E. Diehl, *In Search of Faithfulness: Lessons from the Christian Community* (Philadephia: Fortress, 1987).

51. Thomas Peters and Robert H. Waterman Jr., *In Search of Excellence: Lessons from America's Best-Run Companies* (New York: Harper & Row, 1982).

Chapter 5

1. David Clutterbuck, *Doing It Different: Lessons for the Imaginative Manager* (London: Orion Business Books, 1999).

2. See ibid. See also Peter B. Vaill, *Managing as a Performing Art: New Ideas for a World of Chaotic Change* (San Francisco: Jossey-Bass, 1989); and Patricia Pitcher, *The Drama of Leadership* (New York: Wiley, 1997).

3. Daniel Goleman, *Emotional Intelligence* (New York: Bantam Books, 1995); idem, *Working with Emotional Intelligence* (New York: Bantam Books, 1998); and idem, Richard Boyatzis, and Annie McKee, *Primal Leadership: Realizing the Power of Emotional Intelligence* (Boston: Harvard Business School Press, 2002).

4. Carlos Raimundo, *Relational Capital: True Success through Coaching and Managing Relationships in Business and Life* (Sydney: Prentice-Hall, 2002).

5. Alistair Mant, *Intelligent Leadership* (Sydney: Allen and Unwin, 1997).

6. See John Dalla Costa, *Working Wisdom: The Ultimate Value in the New Economy* (Toronto: Stoddart, 1995).

7. Peter Koestenbaum, *Leadership: The Inner Side of Greatness* (San Francisco: Jossey-Bass, 1991).

8. Patricia La Barre, "Do You Have the Will to Lead?" *Fast Company* 32 (March 2000): 222.

9. James M. Kouzes and Barry Z. Posner, "Seven Lessons for Leading the Voyage to the Future," in *The Leader of the Future: New Visions, Strategies, and Practices for the Next Era*, ed. Frances Hesselbein, Marshall Goldsmith, and Richard Beckhard (San Francisco: Jossey-Bass, 1996), 102–3.

10. Helen J. Alford and Michael J. Naughton, *Managing as If Faith Mattered: Christian Social Principles in the Modern Organization* (Notre Dame, Ind.: University of Notre Dame Press, 2001), 70–96. See further Alasdair MacIntyre, *After Virtue: A Study in Moral Theory*, 2d ed. (Notre Dame, Ind.: University of Notre Dame Press, 1984); and Stanley Hauerwas, *Vision and Virtue: Essays in Christian Ethical Reflection* (Notre Dame, Ind.: University of Notre Dame Press, 1974).

11. Robert N. Bellah, *Habits of the Heart: Individualism and Commitment in American Life* (New York: Harper & Row, 1985); and Stephen R. Covey, *The Seven Habits of Highly Effective People: Restoring the Character Ethic* (New York: Simon & Schuster, 1989).

12. Max De Pree, *Leading without Power: Finding Hope in Serving Community* (San Francisco: Jossey-Bass, 1997), 127, 129.

13. James M. Kouzes and Barry Z. Posner, *Credibility: How Leaders Gain and Lose It, Why People Demand It* (San Francisco: Jossey-Bass, 1993).

14. Frederick F. Reichheld with Thomas Teal, *The Loyalty Effect: The Hidden Force Behind Growth, Profits, and Lasting Value* (Boston: Harvard Business School Press, 2001), 303–4.

15. Gordon Pearson, *Integrity in Organizations: An Alternative Business Ethic* (New York: McGraw-Hill, 1995).

16. Jill W. Graham, "Servant-Leadership and Enterprise Strategy," in *Insights on Leadership: Service, Stewardship, Spirit, and Servant-Leadership*, ed. Larry C. Spears (New York: Wiley, 1998), esp. 151–55.

17. Stephen Carter, *Integrity* (New York: Basic Books, 1996), 5–6.

18. Robert C. Solomon, *Ethics and Excellence: Cooperation and Integrity in Business* (New York: Oxford University Press, 1992), 168.

19. Richard Higginson, *Transforming Leadership: A Christian Approach to Management* (London: SPCK, 1996), 58.

20. Donald B. Kraybill and Phyllis Pellman Good, eds., *Perils of Professionalism: Essays on Christian Faith and Professionalism* (Scottdale, Pa.: Herald Press, 1982).

21. See James A. Autry, *Love and Profit: The Art of Caring Leadership* (New York: Morrow, 1991).

22. Dietrich Bonhoeffer, *Ethics* (London: SCM, 1986), 67, 125–43.

23. Robert K. Greenleaf, "Life's Choices and Markers," in *Reflections on Leadership: How Robert K. Greenleaf's Theory of Servant-Leadership Influenced Today's Top Management Thinkers*, ed. Larry C. Spears (New York: Wiley, 1995), 17–20. This appears in Greenleaf's seminal essay, *The Servant as Leader* (Indianapolis: Robert K. Greenleaf Center, 1970), partly reprinted in Larry C. Spears, ed., *Insights on Leadership: Service, Stewardship, Spirit, and Servant-Leadership* (New York: Wiley, 1998), 15–20; and more fully in Robert K. Greenleaf, *Servant Leadership: A Journey into the Nature of Legitimate Power and Greatness* (New York: Paulist Press, 1977).

24. Richard P. Nielsen, "Quaker Foundations for Greenleaf's Servant Leadership and 'Friendly Disentangling' Method," in *Insights on Leadership*, 126–44.

25. Robert K. Greenleaf, *Seeker and Servant: Reflections on Religious Leadership* (San Francisco: Jossey-Bass, 1996).

26. Anne Fraker, "Robert K. Greenleaf and Business Ethics," in *Insights on Leadership*, 37.

27. Joseph J. DiStefano, "Tracing the Vision and Impact of Robert K. Greenleaf," in *Insights on Leadership*, 63.

28. See Greenleaf, *Servant Leadership*, 28–29.

29. Ibid., 186.

30. Ibid., 29–30, 81.

31. Spears, *Reflections on Leadership*, 4–7; and Joe Batten, "Servant-Leadership: A Passion to Serve," in *Insights on Leadership*, 47–60.

32. Walter C. Wright, *Relational Leadership: A Biblical Model for Leadership Service* (Exeter, Eng.: Paternoster, 2000), 13–17.

33. Peter Block, *The Empowered Manager* (San Francisco: Jossey-Bass, 1987).

34. Peter Block, *Stewardship: Choosing Service over Self-Interest* (San Francisco: Berrett-Koehler, 1993).

35. Ibid., xx.

36. Peter Block, "Stewardship: From Leadership to Citizenship," in *Insights on Leadership*, 88.

37. Ken Blanchard, "Servant-Leadership Revisited," in *Insights on Leadership*, 27.

38. Robert K. Greenleaf, *Old Age: The Ultimate Test of Spirit* (Indianapolis: Robert K. Greenleaf Center, 1987), 2.

39. See Robert K. Greenleaf, *Spirituality and Leadership* (Indianapolis: Robert K. Greenleaf Center, 1988).

40. Shirley Roels, *Moving beyond Servant Leadership* (Pasadena, Calif.: De Pree Leadership Center, 1999).

41. Eugene Peterson, "Follow the Leader," *Fuller Focus* (fall 2001): 31.

Chapter 6

1. Garth Lean, *On the Tail of a Comet: The Life of Frank Buchman* (Colorado Springs: Helmers & Howard, 1988), 43.

2. Ibid., 2.

3. Henry van Dusen, "Apostle to the Twentieth Century," *Atlantic Monthly,* July 1934, 1–2.

4. Cf. Lean, *On the Tail of a Comet,* 461.

5. Peter Howard, *Frank Buchman's Secret* (London: Heinemann, 1961), 13.

6. Lean, *On the Tail of a Comet,* 175.

7. Frank Buchman, New Year's address, 1943.

8. John A. Gates, *The Life and Work of Kierkegaard for Everyman* (London: Hodder & Stoughton, 1960), 141.

9. Bob Buford, *Halftime: Changing Your Game Plan from Success to Significance* (Grand Rapids: Zondervan, 1994).

10. Janet O. Hagberg and Robert A. Guelich, *The Critical Journey: Stages in the Life of Faith* (Dallas: Word, 1990), 21.

11. Ibid., 23.

12. Janet O. Hagberg and Richard J. Leider, *The Inventurers: Excursions in Life and Career Renewal,* 3d ed. (Reading, Mass.: Addison-Wesley, 1982).

13. Janet O. Hagberg, *Real Power: The Stages of Personal Power in Organizations* (Minneapolis: Winston, 1984), viii.

14. Henri J. M. Nouwen. *In the Name of Jesus: Reflections on Christian Leadership* (New York: Crossroad, 1995), 59–60.

15. Robert K. Greenleaf, *Servant Leadership: A Journey into the Nature of Legitimate Power and Greatness* (New York: Paulist Press, 1977), 13.

16. Elizabeth O'Connor, *Call to Commitment: The Story of the Church of the Savior, Washington, D.C.* (New York: Harper & Row, 1963), 13.

17. Elizabeth O'Connor, *The New Community* (New York: Harper & Row, 1976), 91–92.

18. O'Connor, *Call to Commitment,* 5.

19. Ibid., 109.

20. Ibid., 42, 86.

21. Max De Pree, *Does Leadership Have a Future? Questions and Stories for Leaders* (Pasadena, Calif.: De Pree Leadership Center, 2000).

22. Ibid., 14–15.

Conclusion

1. Max De Pree, "Leaving a Legacy" (speech given at the De Pree Leadership Center, Pasadena, Calif., 3 March 1997).

2. Max De Pree, *Leading without Power: Finding Hope in Serving Community* (San Francisco: Jossey-Bass, 1997), 166–75.

bibliography

Alford, Helen J., and Michael J. Naughton. *Managing as If Faith Mattered: Christian Social Principles in the Modern Organization.* Notre Dame, Ind.: University of Notre Dame Press, 2001.

Aubrey, Robert, and Paul M. Cohen. *Working Wisdom.* San Francisco: Jossey-Bass, 1995.

Autry, James A. *Confessions of an Accidental Businessman.* San Francisco: Berrett-Koehler, 1996.

———. *Life and Work: A Manager's Search for Meaning.* New York: Morrow, 1994.

———. *Love and Profit: The Art of Caring Leadership.* New York: Morrow, 1991.

———, and Stephen Mitchell. *Real Power: Business Lessons from the Tao Te Ching.* New York: Riverhead Books, 1998.

Badaracco, Joseph. *Leadership and the Quest of Integrity.* Boston: Harvard Business School Press, 1989.

Banks, Robert, ed. *Faith Goes to Work: Reflections from the Marketplace.* Washington, D.C.: Alban Institute, 1993.

———. *Paul's Idea of Community: The Early House Churches in Their Historical Setting.* Peabody, Mass.: Hendrickson, 1994.

Baron, David, and Lynette Padwa. *Moses on Management: Fifty Leadership Lessons from the Greatest Manager of All Time.* New York: Pocket Books, 1999.

Barton, Bruce. *The Man Nobody Knows.* Indianapolis: Bobbs-Merrill, 1925.

Bass, Bernard M. *Leadership and Performance beyond Expectations.* New York: Free Press, 1985.

————. *Transformational Leadership: Industrial, Military, and Educational Impact.* Mahwah, N.J.: Lawrence Earlbaum, 1998.

Batten, Joe D. *Tough-Minded Leadership.* New York: Amacom, 1989.

Bavinck, Herman. *Our Reasonable Faith: A Survey of Christian Doctrine.* Grand Rapids: Eerdmans, 1956.

Beckett, John. *Loving Monday.* Downers Grove, Ill.: InterVarsity, 1998.

Beckhard, Richard. *Changing the Essence.* San Francisco: Jossey-Bass, 1992.

Belasco, James A. *Teaching the Elephant to Dance.* New York: Plume, 1990.

Bellah, Robert N. *Habits of the Heart: Individualism and Commitment in American Life.* New York: Harper & Row, 1985.

Below, Patrick J., George L. Morrisey, and Betty L. Acomb. *The Executive Guide to Strategic Planning.* San Francisco: Jossey-Bass, 1987.

Benfari, Robert. *Understanding and Changing Your Management Style.* San Francisco: Jossey-Bass, 1999.

Bennis, Warren. *On Becoming a Leader.* Reading, Mass.: Addison-Wesley, 1989.

————. *Why Leaders Can't Lead: The Unconscious Conspiracy Continues.* San Francisco: Jossey-Bass, 1989.

————, and Joan Goldsmith. *Learning to Lead.* Reading, Mass.: Addison-Wesley, 1994.

————, and Burt Nanus. *Leaders: Strategies for Taking Charge.* Rev. ed. New York: Harper & Row, 1997.

————, Jagdish Parikh, and Ronnie Lessem. *Beyond Leadership: Balancing Economics, Ethics, and Ecology.* Oxford: Blackwell, 1994.

Benton, Debra A. *Secrets of a CEO Coach: Your Personal Training Guide to Thinking like a Leader and Acting like a CEO.* New York: McGraw-Hill, 1999.

Blake, Robert R., and Jane S. Mouton. *The Managerial Grid III: A New Look at the Classic That Has Boosted Productivity and Profits for Thousands of Corporations Worldwide.* Houston: Gulf, 1985.

Blanchard, Kenneth, Bill Hybels, and Phil Hodges. *Leadership by the Book: Tools to Transform Your Workplace.* New York: Morrow, 1999.

Blanchard, Kenneth, and Terry Waghorn. *Mission Possible: Becoming a World-Class Organization While There's Still Time.* New York: McGraw-Hill, 1997.

Block, Peter. *The Empowered Manager.* San Francisco: Jossey-Bass, 1987.

————. *Stewardship: Choosing Service over Self-Interest.* San Francisco: Berrett-Koehler, 1993.

————, and Peter Koestenbaum. *Freedom and Accountability at Work: Applying Philosophical Insight to the Real World*. San Francisco: Jossey-Bass, 2001.

Bolles, Richard Nelson. *What Color Is Your Parachute?* San Francisco: Berrett-Koehler, 1993.

Bolman, Lee G., and Terrence E. Deal. *Leading with Soul: An Uncommon Journey of Spirit*. San Francisco: Jossey-Bass, 1995.

————. *Reframing Organizations*. San Francisco: Jossey-Bass, 1991.

Bouque, E. Grady. *The Enemies of Leadership: Lessons for Leaders in Education*. Bloomington, Ind.: Phi Delta Kappa Educational Foundation, 1985.

————. *Leadership by Design: Strengthening Integrity in Higher Education*. San Francisco: Jossey-Bass, 1994.

Boyett, Joseph H., and Jimmie T. Boyett. *The Guru Guide: The Best Ideas of the Top Management Thinkers*. New York: Wiley, 1998.

Bracey, Hyler, Jack Rosenblum, Aubrey Sanford, and Roy Trueblood. *Managing from the Heart*. New York: Delacorte Press, 1990.

Brim, Gilbert. *Ambition: How We Manage Success and Failure throughout Our Lives*. New York: Basic Books, 1992.

Briskin, Alan. *The Stirring of Soul in the Workplace*. San Francisco: Jossey-Bass, 1996.

Brown, Patricia D. *Learning to Lead from Your Spiritual Center*. Nashville: Abingdon, 1996.

Bryman, Alan. *Charisma and Leadership in Organizations*. London: Sage, 1992.

Bryson, John M., and Barbara C. Crosby. *Leadership for the Common Good: Tackling Public Problems in a Shared-Power World*. San Francisco: Jossey-Bass, 1992.

Buford, Bob. *Halftime: Changing Your Game Plan from Success to Significance*. Grand Rapids: Zondervan, 1994.

Burns, James MacGregor. *Leadership*. New York: Harper & Row, 1978.

Cairnes, Margot. *Approaching the Corporate Heart: Breaking through to New Horizons of Personal and Professional Success*. New York: Simon & Schuster, 1998.

Callahan, Kennon L. *Effective Church Leadership: Building on the Twelve Keys*. San Francisco: Harper & Row, 1990.

Carter, Stephen L. *Integrity*. New York: Basic Books, 1996.

Chait, Richard P., Thomas P. Holland, and Barbara E. Taylor. *The Effective Board of Trustees*. Phoenix: Oryx Press, 1993.

Champy, James. *Reengineering Management: The Mandate for New Leadership.* New York: HarperBusiness, 1995.

————, and Nitin Nohria. *The Arc of Ambition: Defining the Leadership Journey.* Cambridge, Mass.: Perseus Books, 2000.

Chappell, Tom. *The Soul of a Business: Managing for Profit and the Common Good.* New York: Bantam Books, 1993.

Childress, John R., and Larry E. Senn. *In the Eye of the Storm: Reengineering Corporate Culture.* Los Angeles: Leadership Press, 1995.

Clark, Kenneth E., and Miriam B. Clark, eds. *Measures of Leadership.* West Orange, N.J.: Leadership Library of America, 1990.

Clawson, James G. *Level Three Leadership: Getting Below the Surface.* 2d ed. Upper Saddle River, N.J.: Prentice-Hall, 1999.

Clinton, J. Robert. *The Making of a Leader: Recognizing the Lessons and Stages of Leadership Development.* Colorado Springs: NavPress, 1988.

————. *A Short History of Leadership.* Altadena, Calif.: Barnabas Publishers, 1992.

Clutterbuck, David. *Doing It Different: Lessons for the Imaginative Manager.* London: Orion Business Books, 1999.

Cohen, Allan R., and David L. Bradford. *Influence without Authority.* New York: Wiley, 1990.

Coles, Robert. *The Call of Service: A Witness to Idealism.* Boston: Houghton-Mifflin, 1993.

Collins, James C., and Jerry I. Porras. *Built to Last: Successful Habits of Visionary Companies.* New York: HarperBusiness, 1994.

Conger, Jay A. *The Charismatic Leader: Behind the Mystique of Exceptional Leadership.* San Francisco: Jossey-Bass, 1989.

————. *Learning to Lead: The Art of Transforming Managers into Leaders.* San Francisco: Jossey-Bass, 1992.

————, ed. *Spirit at Work: Discovering the Spirituality in Leadership.* San Francisco: Jossey-Bass, 1994.

————, and Beth Benjamin. *Building Leaders: How Successful Companies Develop the Next Generation.* San Francisco: Jossey-Bass, 1999.

————, Gretchen M. Spreitzer, and Edward E. Lawler III, eds. *The Leader's Change Handbook: An Essential Guide to Setting Direction and Taking Action.* San Francisco: Jossey-Bass, 1999.

Covey, Stephen R. *Principle-Centered Leadership*. New York: Summit Books, 1991.

————. *The Seven Habits of Highly Effective People: Restoring the Character Ethic*. New York: Simon & Schuster, 1989.

————, A. Roger Merrill, and Rebecca R. Merrill. *First Things First: To Live, to Love, to Learn, to Leave a Legacy*. New York: Simon & Schuster, 1994.

Cox, Danny, with John Hoover. *Leadership When the Heat's On*. New York: McGraw-Hill, 1992.

Cramer, Kathryn D. *Staying on Top When Your World Turns Upside Down: How to Triumph over Trauma and Adversity*. New York: Viking, 1990.

Crocker, H. W., III. *Robert E. Lee on Leadership: Executive Lessons in Character, Courage, and Vision*. Rocklin, Calif.: Forum, 1999.

Dale, Robert D. *Good News from Great Leaders*. Washington, D.C.: Alban Institute, 1992.

Dalla Costa, John. *Working Wisdom: The Ultimate Value in the New Economy*. Toronto: Stoddart, 1995.

Dattner, Fabian, Jim Luscombe, and Kenneth Grant. *Three Spirits of Leadership: The United Voice of the Entrepreneur, the Corporation, and the Community*. Crows Nest, Austral.: Allen & Unwin, 1999.

De Pree, Max. *Leadership Is an Art*. New York: Doubleday, 1989.

————. *Leadership Jazz*. New York: Currency Doubleday, 1992.

————. *Leading without Power: Finding Hope in Serving Community*. San Francisco: Jossey-Bass, 1997.

De Vries, Manfred F. R. Kets. *Life and Death in the Executive Fast Lane: Essays on Irrational Organizations and Their Leaders*. San Francisco: Jossey-Bass, 1995.

————. *Prisoners of Leadership*. New York: Wiley, 1989.

Diehl, William E. *In Search of Faithfulness: Lessons from the Christian Community*. Philadelphia: Fortress, 1987.

————. *The Monday Connection: A Spirituality of Competence, Affirmation, and Support in the Workplace*. San Francisco: HarperSanFrancisco, 1991.

Doohan, Helen. *Leadership in Paul*. Wilmington, Del.: Michael Glazier, 1984.

Drath, Wilfred H., and Charles J. Palus. *Making Common Sense: Leadership as Meaning-Making in a Community of Practice*. Greensboro, N.C.: Center for Creative Leadership, 1994.

Drucker, Peter F. *The Effective Executive*. New York: Harper & Row, 1967.

————. *Innovation and Entrepreneurship: Practice and Principles*. New York: Harper & Row, 1985.

————. *Management Challenges for the Twenty-First Century*. New York: Harper-Business, 1999.

————. *Managing in Turbulent Times*. New York: Harper & Row, 1980.

Dunphy, Dexter, and Andrew Griffiths. *The Sustainable Corporation: Organisational Renewal in Australia*. Sydney: Allen & Unwin, 1999.

Edelman, Joel, and Mary Beth Crain. *The Tao of Negotiation: How You Can Prevent, Resolve, and Transcend Conflict in Work and Everyday Life*. New York: HarperBusiness, 1993.

Egan, Gerard. *Adding Value: A Systematic Guide to Business-Driven Management and Leadership*. San Francisco: Jossey-Bass, 1993.

Engstrom, Ted W., and Edward R. Dayton. *The Art of Management for Christian Leaders*. Grand Rapids: Pyranee Books, 1989.

Evans, John S. *The Management of Human Capacity: An Approach to the Ideas of Elliott Jacques*. Bradford, Eng.: MCB Human Resources, 1979.

Farson, Richard. *Management of the Absurd: Paradoxes in Leadership*. New York: Simon & Schuster, 1996.

Fiedler, Fred E. *A Theory of Leadership Effectiveness*. New York: McGraw-Hill, 1967.

Finzel, Hans. *The Top Ten Mistakes Leaders Make*. Wheaton: Victor Books, 1994.

Fisher, Roger, and William Ury. *Getting to Yes: Negotiating Agreement without Giving In*. New York: Penguin Books, 1993.

Fitzgerald, Catherine, and Linda K. Kirby, eds. *Developing Leaders: Research and Applications in Psychological Type and Leadership Development*. Palo Alto, Calif.: Davies-Black, 1997.

Flood, Robert Louis. *Rethinking the Fifth Discipline: Learning within the Unknowable*. New York: Routledge, 1999.

Ford, Leighton. *Jesus: The Transforming Leader*. London: Hodder & Stoughton, 1991.

————. *Transforming Leadership: Jesus' Way of Creating Vision, Shaping Values, and Empowering Change*. Downers Grove, Ill.: InterVarsity, 1991.

Fox, Matthew. *The Reinvention of Work: A New Vision of Livelihood for Our Time*. San Francisco: HarperSanFrancisco, 1994.

Fraker, Anne T., and Larry C. Spears, eds. *Seeker and Servant: Reflections on Religious Leadership*. San Francisco: Jossey-Bass, 1996.

Fromm, Bill, and Len Schlesinger. *The Real Heroes of Business and Not a CEO among Them*. New York: Doubleday, 1993.

Fukuyama, Francis. *Trust: The Social Virtues and the Creation of Prosperity*. New York: Free Press, 1995.

Fullan, Michael. *Educational Leadership*. San Francisco: Jossey-Bass, 2000.

Fuller, Timothy, ed. *Leading and Leadership*. Notre Dame, Ind.: University of Notre Dame Press, 2000.

Galpin, Timothy J. *The Human Side of Change: A Practical Guide to Organization Redesign*. San Francisco: Jossey-Bass, 1996.

Gardner, Howard. *Leading Minds: An Anatomy of Leadership*. New York: Basic Books, 1995.

Gardner, John W. *Building Community*. New York: Independent Sector, 1991.

———. *On Leadership*. New York: Free Press, 1990.

Garfield, Charles, with Michael Toms. *The Soul of Business: New Dimensions*. Carlsbad, Calif.: Hay House, 1997.

Gates, John A. *The Life and Work of Kierkegaard for Everyman*. London: Hodder & Stoughton, 1960.

Goldingay, John. *Men Behaving Badly*. Exeter, Eng.: Paternoster, 2000.

Goleman, Daniel. *Emotional Intelligence*. New York: Bantam Books, 1995.

———. *Working with Emotional Intelligence*. New York: Bantam Books, 1998.

———, Richard Boyatzis, and Annie McKee. *Primal Leadership: Realizing the Power of Emotional Intelligence*. Boston: Harvard Business School Press, 2002.

Gouillart, Francis J., and James N. Kelly. *Transforming the Organization*. New York: McGraw-Hill, 1995.

Gozdz, Kazimierz. *Community Building: Renewing Spirit and Learning*. Pleasanton, Calif.: New Leaders Press, 1995.

Greenleaf, Robert K. *Servant Leadership: A Journey into the Nature of Legitimate Power and Greatness*. New York: Paulist Press, 1977.

———, Don M. Frick, and Larry C. Spears, eds. *On Becoming a Servant-Leader*. San Francisco: Jossey-Bass, 1996.

Greenslade, Philip. *Leadership*. London: Marshall Pickering, 1984.

Gregg, Samuel, and Gordon Preece. *Christianity and Entrepreneurship: Protestant and Catholic Thoughts*. Sydney: Centre for Independent Studies, 1999.

Griffin, Emilie. *The Reflective Executive: A Spirituality of Business and Enterprise*. New York: Crossroad, 1993.

Gunderson, Denny. *The Leadership Paradox: A Challenge to Servant Leadership in a Power Hungry World.* Seattle: YWAM, 1997.

Hagberg, Janet O. *Real Power: The Stages of Personal Power in Organizations.* Minneapolis: Winston, 1984.

———, and Richard J. Leider. *The Inventurers: Excursions in Life and Career Renewal.* 3d ed. Reading, Mass.: Addison-Wesley, 1988.

Haggai, John. *Lead On! Leadership That Endures in a Changing World.* Waco: Word, 1986.

Hamilton, Nigel. *Monty: The Making of a General, 1887–1942.* New York: McGraw-Hill, 1981.

Handy, Charles. *The Age of Unreason.* Boston: Harvard Business School Press, 1989.

———. *Beyond Certainty: The Changing Worlds of Organizations.* Boston: Harvard Business School Press, 1996.

———. *Gods of Management: The Changing Work of Organizations.* New York: Oxford University Press, 1995.

———. *The Hungry Spirit: Beyond Capitalism: A Quest for Purpose in the Modern World.* New York: Broadway Books, 1998.

———. *The New Alchemists: How Visionary People Make Something out of Nothing.* London: Hutchinson, 1999.

———. *Understanding Organizations.* New York: Oxford University Press, 1993.

———. *Waiting for the Mountain to Move: Reflections on Work and Life.* San Francisco: Jossey-Bass, 1999.

Hartshorne, Charles. *Reality as Social Process: Studies in Metaphysics and Religion.* Glencoe, Ill.: Free Press, 1953.

Hass, Howard, with Bob Tamarkin. *The Leader Within: An Empowering Path of Self-Discovery.* New York: HarperBusiness, 1992.

Haughey, John C. *Converting 9 to 5: A Spirituality of Daily Work.* New York: Crossroad, 1989.

———. "A Leader's Conscience: The Integrity and Spirituality of Václav Havel." In *Spirit at Work: Discovering the Spirituality in Leadership,* edited by Jay A. Conger. San Francisco: Jossey-Bass, 1994.

Havel, Václav. *Disturbing the Peace: A Conversation with Karel Hvízdala.* Translated by Paul Wilson. New York: Knopf, 1990.

———. *Letters to Olga: June 1979–September 1982.* Translated by Paul Wilson. New York: Holt, 1989.

Hawley, Jack. *Reawakening the Spirit in Work: The Power of Dharmic Management.* San Francisco: Berrett-Koehler, 1993.

Heifetz, Ronald A. *Leadership without Easy Answers.* Cambridge: Belknap Press of Harvard University Press, 1994.

Helgesen, Sally. *The Female Advantage: Women's Ways of Leadership.* New York: Doubleday Currency, 1990.

————. *The Web of Inclusion: A New Architecture for Building Great Organizations.* New York: Doubleday Currency, 1995.

Hendricks, Gay, and Kate Ludeman. *The Corporate Mystic: A Guidebook for Visionaries with Their Feet on the Ground.* New York: Bantam Books, 1996.

Hersey, Paul, Kenneth H. Blanchard, and Dewey E. Johnson. *Management of Organizational Behavior: Utilizing Human Resources.* Upper Saddle River, N.J.: Prentice-Hall, 1996.

Hess, J. Daniel. *Integrity: Let Your Yea Be Yea.* Scottdale, Pa.: Herald Press, 1978.

Hesselbein, Frances, Marshall Goldsmith, and Richard Beckhard, eds. *The Leader of the Future: New Visions, Strategies, and Practices for the Next Era.* San Francisco: Jossey-Bass, 1996.

————, eds. *The Organization of the Future.* San Francisco: Jossey-Bass, 1997.

————, and Richard Schubert, eds. *The Community of the Future.* San Francisco: Jossey-Bass, 1998.

Hickman, Craig R. *Mind of a Manager, Soul of a Leader.* New York: Wiley, 1990.

Higginson, Richard. *Transforming Leadership: A Christian Approach to Management.* London: SPCK, 1996.

Hillman, James. *The Soul's Code: In Search of Character and Calling.* New York: Random House, 1996.

Hodgkinson, Christopher. *The Philosophy of Leadership.* New York: St. Martin's Press, 1983.

Holmes, Arthur F. *Shaping Character: Moral Education in the Christian College.* Grand Rapids: Eerdmans, 1991.

Howard, Peter. *Frank Buchman's Secret.* London: Heinemann, 1961.

Hughes, Richard L., Robert C. Ginnett, and Gordon J. Curphy. *Leadership: Enhancing the Lessons of Experience.* 2d ed. Chicago: Irwin, 1996.

Huszczo, Gregory E. *Tools for Team Excellence: Getting Your Team into High Gear and Keeping It There.* Palo Alto, Calif.: Davies-Black, 1996.

Hybels, Bill. "Finding Your Leadership Style: Ten Different Ways to Lead God's People." *Leadership* (winter 1998): 84–89.

Hyland, Bruce N., and Merle J. Yost. *Reflections for Managers.* New York: McGraw-Hill, 1994.

Jacobsen, Steve. *Hearts to God, Hands to Work: Connecting Spirituality and Work.* Washington, D.C.: Alban Institute, 1997.

James, Jennifer. *Thinking in the Future Tense: Leadership Skills for a New Age.* New York: Simon & Schuster, 1996.

Janov, Jill. *The Inventive Organization: Hope and Daring at Work.* San Francisco: Jossey-Bass, 1994.

Jaworski, Joseph. *Synchronicity: The Inner Path of Leadership.* San Francisco: Berrett-Koehler, 1996.

Jinkins, Michael, and Deborah Bradshaw Jinkins. *The Character of Leadership: Political Realism and Public Virtue in Nonprofit Organizations.* San Francisco: Jossey-Bass, 1998.

Johnson, Barry. *Polarity Management: Identifying and Managing Unsolvable Problems.* Amherst, Mass.: HRD Press, 1992.

Jones, Laura Beth. *Jesus CEO: Using Ancient Wisdom for Visionary Leadership.* New York: Hyperion, 1995.

———. *The Path.* New York: Hyperion, 1996.

Kanter, Rosabeth Moss. *Rosabeth Moss Kanter on the Frontiers of Management.* Boston: Harvard Business School Press, 1997.

———, Barry A. Stein, and Todd D. Jick. *The Challenge of Organizational Change: How Companies Experience It and Leaders Guide It.* New York: Free Press, 1992.

Keating, Charles J. *The Leadership Book.* Rev. ed. New York: Paulist Press, 1982.

Kerr, Alan. *Guided Journey.* Gundaroo, Austral.: Brolga Press, 1998.

Koestenbaum, Peter. *Leadership: The Inner Side of Greatness.* San Francisco: Jossey-Bass, 1991.

Kotter, John P. *A Force for Change: How Leadership Differs from Management.* New York: Free Press, 1990.

———. *The New Rules: How to Succeed in Today's Post-Corporate World.* New York: Free Press, 1995.

Kouzes, James M., and Barry Z. Posner. *Credibility: How Leaders Gain and Lose It, Why People Demand It.* San Francisco: Jossey-Bass, 1993.

————. *The Leadership Challenge.* 3d ed. San Francisco: Jossey-Bass, 2002.

Kraybill, Donald B., and Phyllis Pellman Good, eds. *Perils of Professionalism: Essays on Christian Faith and Professionalism.* Scottdale, Pa.: Herald Press, 1982.

Kundtz, David. *Stopping.* New York: MJF Books, 1998.

LaCugna, Catherine Mowry. *God for Us: The Trinity and Christian Life.* San Francisco: HarperCollins, 1993.

Lean, Garth. *On the Tail of a Comet: The Life of Frank Buchman.* Colorado Springs: Helmers & Howard, 1988.

Leider, Richard J. *The Power of Purpose: Creating Meaning in Your Life and Work.* San Francisco: Berrett-Koehler, 1997.

Lencioni, Patrick. *The Five Temptations of a CEO: A Leadership Fable.* San Francisco: Jossey-Bass, 1998.

Le Peau, Andrew T. *Paths of Leadership: Guiding Others toward Growth in Christ through Serving, Following, Teaching, Modeling, Envisioning.* Downers Grove, Ill.: InterVarsity, 1983.

Lipman-Blumen, Jean. *The Connective Edge: Leading in an Independent World.* San Francisco: Jossey-Bass, 1996.

Lynch, Richard. *Lead! How Public and Nonprofit Managers Can Bring Out the Best in Themselves and Their Organizations.* San Francisco: Jossey-Bass, 1993.

Mallison, John. *Mentoring to Develop Disciples and Leaders.* Sydney: Scripture Union/Open Book, 1998.

Mant, Alistair. *Intelligent Leadership.* Crows Nest, Austral.: Allen & Unwin, 1997.

Manz, Charles C. *The Leadership Wisdom of Jesus: Practical Lessons for Today.* San Francisco: Berrett-Koehler, 1998.

————, and Henry P. Simms. *Superleadership: Leading Others to Lead Themselves.* Don Mills, Ont.: Pearson Education Canada, 1989.

Marcic, Dorothy. *Managing with Wisdom of Love: Uncovering Virtue in People and Organizations.* San Francisco: Jossey-Bass, 1997.

Maxwell, John C. *Developing the Leader within You.* Nashville: Thomas Nelson, 1993.

————. *The Twenty-One Irrefutable Laws of Leadership: Follow Them and People Will Follow You.* Nashville: Thomas Nelson, 1998.

McCauley, Cynthia D., Russ S. Moxley, and Ellen Van Velsor, eds. *The Center for Creative Leadership Handbook of Leadership Development.* San Francisco: Jossey-Bass, 1998.

Melrose, Ken. *Making the Grass Greener on Your Side: A CEO's Journey to Leading by Serving.* San Francisco: Berrett-Koehler, 1995.

Mitroff, Ian I., and Elizabeth A. Denton. *A Spiritual Audit of Corporate America: A Hard Look at Spirituality, Religion, and Values in the Workplace.* San Francisco: Jossey-Bass, 1999.

Mohrman, Allan M., Jr., Susan Albers Mohrman, and Gerald E. Ledford. *Large-Scale Organizational Change.* San Francisco: Jossey-Bass, 1989.

Morgan, Gareth. *Images of Organization.* London: Sage, 1986.

Moxley, Russ S. *Leadership and Spirit: Breathing New Vitality and Energy into Individuals and Organizations.* San Francisco: Jossey-Bass, 2000.

Nader, Jonar C. *How to Lose Friends and Infuriate People.* Cherrybrook, Austral.: Plutonium, 1999.

Nair, Keshavan. *A Higher Standard of Leadership: Lessons from the Life of Gandhi.* San Francisco: Berrett-Koehler, 1994.

Naisbitt, John, and Patricia Aburdene. *Megatrends 2000: Ten New Directions for the 1990s.* New York: Morrow, 1990.

Nanus, Burt. *The Leader's Edge: The Seven Keys to Leadership in a Turbulent World.* Chicago: Contemporary Books, 1989.

―――. *Visionary Leadership.* San Francisco: Jossey-Bass, 1992.

Nash, Laura L. *Believers in Business.* Nashville: Thomas Nelson, 1994.

―――, and Scotty McLennan. *Church on Sunday, Work on Monday: The Challenge of Fusing Christian Values with Business Life.* San Francisco: Jossey-Bass, 2001.

Nix, William H. *Character Works.* Nashville: Broadman & Holman, 1999.

Northouse, Peter G. *Leadership: Theory and Practice.* 3d ed. Thousand Oaks, Calif.: Sage, 2004.

Novak, Michael. *Business as a Calling: Work and the Examined Life.* New York: Free Press, 1996.

Oakley, Ed, and Doug Krug. *Enlightened Leadership: Getting to the Heart of Change.* New York: Simon & Schuster, 1994.

O'Connor, Elizabeth. *Call to Commitment: The Story of the Church of the Savior, Washington, D.C.* New York: Harper & Row, 1963.

Orsborn, Carol. *Inner Excellence: Spiritual Principles of Life-Driven Business.* San Rafael, Calif.: New World Library, 1992.

O'Toole, James. *Leading Change: Overcoming the Ideology of Comfort and the Tyranny of Custom.* San Francisco: Jossey-Bass, 1995.

Palmer, Parker J. *The Active Life: A Spirituality of Work, Creativity, and Caring.* San Francisco: Harper & Row, 1990.

—. *Leading from Within: Reflections on Spirituality and Leadership.* Washington, D.C.: Servant Leadership School, 1990.

—. *The Promise of Paradox: A Celebration of Contradictions in the Christian Life.* Washington, D.C.: Servant Leadership School, 1993.

Parker, Glenn M. *Team Players and Teamwork: The New Competitive Business Strategy.* San Francisco: Jossey-Bass, 1990.

Pascale, Richard Tanner. *Managing on the Edge: How the Smartest Companies Use Conflict to Stay Ahead.* New York: Simon & Schuster, 1990.

Pascarella, Perry. *Christ-Centered Leadership: Thriving in Business by Putting God in Charge.* Rocklin, Calif.: Prima, 1999.

Pattison, Stephen. *The Faith of the Managers: When Management Becomes Religion.* London: Cassell, 1997.

—. "Recognizing Leaders' Hidden Beliefs." In *Faith and Leadership: How Leaders Live Out Their Faith in Their Work and Why It Matters.* Edited by Robert Banks and Kim Powell. San Francisco: Jossey-Bass, 2000.

Pearce, Terry. *Leading Out Loud: The Authentic Speaker, the Credible Leader.* San Francisco: Jossey-Bass, 1995.

Pearman, Roger R. *Hard Wired Leadership: Unleashing the Power of Personality to Become a New Millennium Leader.* Palo Alto, Calif.: Davies-Black, 1998.

Pearson, Gordon. *Integrity in Organizations: An Alternative Business Ethic.* New York: McGraw-Hill, 1995.

Perkins, Dennis N. T. *Leading at the Edge: Leadership Lessons from the Extraordinary Saga of Shackleton's Antarctic Expedition.* New York: Amacom, 2000.

Peters, Thomas. *Liberation Management: Necessary Disorganization for the Nanosecond Nineties.* New York: Knopf, 1992.

—. "Rule #3: Leadership Is as Confusing as Hell." *Fast Company* 44 (March 2001): 124–40.

—. *Thriving on Chaos: Handbook for a Management Revolution.* New York: Knopf, 1987.

—, and Robert H. Waterman Jr. *In Search of Excellence: Lessons from America's Best-Run Companies.* New York: Harper & Row, 1982.

Peterson, Linda. *Starting Out, Starting Over: Finding the Work That's Waiting for You.* Palo Alto, Calif.: Davies-Black. 1995.

Phillips, Donald T. *Lincoln on Leadership: Executive Strategies for Tough Times.* New York: Warner Books, 1992.

Pierce, Gregory F. A. *Spirituality at Work: Ten Ways to Balance Your Life on the Job.* Chicago: Loyola, 2001.

Pinchot, Gifford. *Creating Organizations with Many Leaders.* San Francisco: Jossey-Bass, 1996.

————, and Elizabeth Pinchot. *The End of Bureaucracy and the Rise of the Intelligent Organization.* San Francisco: Berrett-Koehler, 1993.

Pitcher, Patricia. *The Drama of Leadership.* New York: Wiley, 1997.

Pollard, C. William. *The Soul of the Firm.* New York: HarperBusiness, 1996.

Powell, James Lawrence. *Pathways to Leadership: How to Achieve and Sustain Success.* San Francisco: Jossey-Bass, 1995.

Preece, Gordon. *A Trinitarian Perspective on Work.* New York: Edward Mellen, 1998.

Quinn, Robert E. *Beyond Rational Management: Mastering the Paradoxes and Competing Demands of High Performance.* San Francisco: Jossey-Bass, 1988.

————. *Deep Change: Discovering the Leader Within.* San Francisco: Jossey-Bass, 1996.

Raimundo, Carlos. *Relational Capital: True Success through Coaching and Managing Relationships in Business and Life.* Sydney: Prentice-Hall, 2002.

Reichheld, Frederick F., with Thomas Teal. *The Loyalty Effect: The Hidden Force Behind Growth, Profits, and Lasting Value.* Boston: Harvard Business School Press, 2001.

Renesch, John. *Leadership in a New Era: Visionary Perspectives on the Big Issues of Our Time.* San Francisco: New Leaders Press, 1994.

————, ed. *New Traditions in Business: Spirit and Leadership in the Twenty-First Century.* San Francisco: Berrett-Koehler, 1992.

Reynolds, Joe. *Out Front Leadership: Discovering, Developing, and Delivering Your Potential.* Austin, Tex.: Mott & Carlisle, 1993.

Rinehart, Stacy T. *Upside Down: The Paradox of Servant Leadership.* Colorado Springs: NavPress, 1998.

Rion, Michael. *The Responsible Manager: Practical Strategies for Ethical Decision Making.* San Francisco: Harper & Row, 1990.

Sakenfeld, Katharine Doob. *Faithfulness in Action: Loyalty in Biblical Perspective.* Philadelphia: Fortress, 1985.

Salkin, Jeffrey K. *Being God's Partner: How to Find the Hidden Link between Spirituality and Your Work.* Woodstock, Vt.: Jewish Lights Publishing, 1994.

Sanders, J. Oswald. *Paul the Leader: A Vision for Christian Leadership Today.* Eastbourne, Eng.: Kingsway, 1983.

———. *Spiritual Leadership.* Rev. ed. Chicago: Moody, 1980.

Sarros, John C., and Oleh Butchatsky. *Leadership: Australia's Top CEOs: Finding Out What Makes Them the Best.* New York: HarperBusiness, 1996.

Sayers, Dorothy L. *The Mind of the Maker.* London: Methuen, 1941.

Schaef, Anne Wilson, and Diane Fassel. *The Addictive Organization.* San Francisco: Harper & Row, 1988.

Schein, Edgar H. *The Corporate Culture Survival Guide: Sense and Nonsense about Culture Change.* San Francisco: Jossey-Bass, 1999.

———. *Organizational Culture and Leadership.* 2d ed. San Francisco: Jossey-Bass, 1992.

Schumacher, Christian. *God in Work: Discovering the Divine Pattern for Work in the New Millennium.* Oxford, Eng.: Lion Publishing, 1998.

———. *To Live and Work: A Theological Interpretation.* Bromley, Eng.: Marc, 1987.

Schwartz, Peter. *The Art of the Long View: Planning for the Future in an Uncertain World.* New York: Currency Doubleday, 1995.

Senge, Peter M. *The Fifth Discipline: The Art and Practice of the Learning Organization.* New York: Doubleday Currency, 1990.

Sennett, Richard. *The Corrosion of Character: The Personal Consequences of Work in the New Capitalism.* New York: Norton, 1998.

Simon, Sidney B., Leland W. Howe, and Howard Kirschenbaum. *Values Clarification.* Rev. ed. New York: Warner Books, 1995.

Sinclair, Amanda. *Doing Leadership Differently: Gender, Power, and Sexuality in a Changing Business Culture.* Victoria, Austral.: Melbourne University Press, 1998.

Sinetar, Marsha. *Do What You Love, the Money Will Follow: Discovering Your Right Livelihood.* New York: Dell, 1989.

Sire, James W. *Václav Havel: The Intellectual Conscience of International Politics: An Introduction, Appreciation, and Critique.* Downers Grove, Ill.: InterVarsity, 2001.

Smedes, Lewis. *Choices: Making Right Decisions in a Complex World.* San Francisco: HarperSanFrancisco, 1991.

Sofield, Loughlan, and Donald H. Kuhn. *The Collaborative Leader: Listening to the Wisdom of God's People.* Notre Dame, Ind.: Ave Maria Press, 1995.

Solomon, Robert C. *Ethics and Excellence: Cooperation and Integrity in Business.* New York: Oxford University Press, 1992.

Spears, Larry C., ed. *Insights on Leadership: Service, Stewardship, Spirit, and Servant-Leadership.* New York: Wiley, 1998.

—————, ed. *Reflections on Leadership: How Robert K. Greenleaf's Theory of Servant-Leadership Influenced Today's Top Management Thinkers.* New York: Wiley, 1995.

Spink, Kathryn. *Mother Teresa: A Complete Authorized Biography.* San Francisco: HarperSanFrancisco, 1997.

Stevens, R. Paul, and Phil Collins. *The Equipping Pastor: A Systems Approach to Congregational Leadership.* Washington, D.C.: Alban Institute, 1993.

Stogdill, Ralph M. *Handbook of Leadership: A Survey of Theory and Research.* New York: Free Press, 1974.

Sullivan, William M. *Work and Integrity: The Crisis and Promise of Professionalism in America.* New York: HarperBusiness, 1995.

Swain, Bernard F. *Liberating Leadership: Practical Styles for Pastoral Ministry.* San Francisco: Harper & Row, 1986.

Swiss, Deborah. *Women Breaking Through: Overcoming the Final Ten Obstacles at Work.* Princeton, N.J.: Peterson's/Pacesetter Books, 1996.

Terry, Robert W. *Authentic Leadership: Courage in Action.* San Francisco: Jossey-Bass, 1993.

Theobald, Robert. *Reworking Success: New Communities at the Millennium.* Gabriola Island, B.C.: New Society Publishers, 1997.

Thrall, Bill, Bruce McElrath, and Jim McNichol. *The Ascent of the Leader: How Ordinary Relationships Develop Extraordinary Character and Influence.* Hoboken, N.J.: Wiley, 1999.

Tomasko, Robert M. *Downsizing: Reshaping the Corporation for the Future.* New York: Amacom, 1990.

Ury, William. *Getting Past No: Negotiating Your Way from Confrontation to Cooperation.* Rev. ed. New York: Bantam Books, 1993.

Vaill, Peter B. *Managing as a Performing Art: New Ideas for a World of Chaotic Change.* San Francisco: Jossey-Bass, 1989.

———. *Spirited Leading and Learning: Process Wisdom for a New Age.* San Francisco: Jossey-Bass, 1998.

Vladilav, J., ed. *Václav Havel, or Living in Truth.* London: Faber & Faber, 1990.

Waterman, Robert H., Jr. *Adhocracy: The Power to Change.* New York: Norton, 1990.

Wheatley, Margaret J. *Leadership and the New Science: Learning about Organization from an Orderly Universe.* San Francisco: Berrett-Koehler, 1992.

White, John. *Excellence in Leadership: Reaching Goals with Prayer, Courage, and Determination.* Downers Grove, Ill.: InterVarsity, 1986.

Whyte, David. *The Heart Aroused: Poetry and the Preservation of the Soul in Corporate America.* New York: Currency Doubleday, 1994.

Wilkins, Alan L. *Developing Corporate Character: How to Successfully Change an Organization without Destroying It.* San Francisco: Jossey-Bass, 1989.

Williams, Benjamin D., and Michael T. McKibben. *Oriented Leadership: Why All Christians Need It.* Wayne, N.J.: Orthodox Christian Publications Center, 1994.

Williams, Oliver F., and John W. Houck, eds. *A Virtuous Life in Business: Stories of Courage and Integrity in the Corporate World.* Lanham, Md.: Rowman & Littlefield, 1992.

Wills, Garry. *Certain Trumpets: The Call of Leaders.* New York: Simon & Schuster, 1994.

Wren, J. Thomas. *The Leader's Companion: Insights on Leadership through the Ages.* New York: Free Press, 1995.

Wright, Walter C. *Relational Leadership: A Biblical Model for Leadership Service.* Exeter, Eng.: Paternoster, 2000.

Yukl, Gary A. *Leadership in Organizations.* 3d ed. Englewood Cliffs, N.J.: Prentice-Hall, 1989.

Zohar, Danah. *Rewiring the Corporate Brain: Using the New Science to Rethink How We Structure and Lead Organizations.* San Francisco: Berrett-Koehler, 1997.

index

Made in the USA
Lexington, KY
17 August 2015